C/C++

PROGRAMMER'S REFERENCE

Herbert Schildt

Osborne **McGraw-Hill**

Berkeley New York St. Louis San Francisco
Auckland Bogotá Hamburg London Madrid
Mexico City Milan Montreal New Delhi Panama City
Paris São Paulo Singapore Sydney
Tokyo Toronto

Osborne **McGraw-Hill**
2600 Tenth Street
Berkeley, California 94710
U.S.A.

For information on translations or book distributors outside of the U.S.A., or to arrange bulk purchase discounts for sales, promotions, premiums, or fundraisers, please write to Osborne **McGraw-Hill** at the above address.

C/C++: Programmer's Reference

Publisher Brandon A. Nordin
Editor in Chief Scott Rogers
Acquisitions Editor Megg Bonar
Technical Editor Greg Guntle
Indexer Sheryl Schildt
Design and Composition Publication Services
Senior Project Coordinator Rhonda Zachmeyer
Copy Editor Thomas A. Long

234567890 DOC 9987

ISBN 0-07-882367-6

CONTENTS

INTRODUCTION

C and C++ are the world's most important programming languages. Indeed, to be a professional programmer today implies proficiency at these two languages. They are the foundation upon which modern programming is built.

C was invented by Dennis Ritchie in the 1970s. C is a middle-level language. It combines the control structures of a high-level language with the ability to manipulate bits, bytes, and pointers (addresses). Thus, C gives the programmer nearly complete control over the machine. C was standardized late in 1989 when the American National Standards Institute (ANSI) standard for C was adopted. This standard was also adopted by ISO (International Standards Organization) in 1990. The C standard was amended slightly in 1996.

C++ was created by Bjarne Stroustrup in the 1980s. It began as a set of object-oriented extensions to C, but it soon expanded into being a programming language in its own right. While C++ is still built upon the foundation of C, its new features nearly double the size of the language. Needless to say, C++ is one of the most powerful computer languages devised to date. An ANSI/ISO standard for C++ is nearing completion, and for all intents and purposes, C++ is a standardized language.

The material in this book describes ANSI standard C and the current version of the C++ standard created by the ANSI/ISO standardization committee.

As you are undoubtedly aware, C and C++ are large topics. It is, of course, not possible to cover every aspect of these important languages here. Instead, this quick reference distills their most salient features into a convenient, easy-to-use form.

Chapter 1—Data Types, Variables, and Constants

C and C++ offer the programmer a rich assortment of built-in data types. Programmer-defined data types can be created to fit virtually any need. Variables can be created for any valid data type. Also, it is possible to specify constants of C/C++'s built-in types. In this chapter, various features relating to data types, variables, and constants are discussed.

THE BASIC TYPES

C defines five basic built-in data types:

Type	Keyword
Character	char
Integer	int
Floating-point	float
Double floating-point	double
Valueless	void

C++ adds two:

Type	Keyword
Boolean (true/false)	bool
Wide-character	wchar_t

Several of the basic types can be modified using one or more of these type modifiers:

signed

unsigned

short

long

Type modifiers precede the type name that they modify. All of the built-in data types, including modifiers, allowed by C and C++ are shown in the following table along with their guaranteed minimum ranges. Most compilers will exceed the minimums for one or more types. Also, if your computer uses two's complement arithmetic (as most do), then the smallest negative value that can be stored by a signed integer will be one more than the minimums shown. For example, the range of an **int** for most computers is −32,768 to 32,767. Whether type **char** is signed or unsigned is implementation-dependent.

Type	Minimum Range
bool	true/false
char	−127 to 127 or 0 to 255
unsigned char	0 to 255
signed char	−127 to 127
int	−32,767 to 32,767
unsigned int	0 to 65,535
signed int	same as int
short int	same as int
unsigned short int	0 to 65,535
signed short int	same as short int
long int	−2,147,483, 647 to 2,147,483,647
signed long int	same as long int
unsigned long int	0 to 4,294,967,295
float	6 digits of precision
double	10 digits of precision
long double	10 digits of precision
wchar_t	same as unsigned int

When a type modifier is used by itself, **int** is assumed. For example, you can specify an unsigned integer by simply using the keyword **unsigned**. Thus, these declarations are equivalent.

```
unsigned int i; // here, int is specified
unsigned i; // here, int is implied
```

DECLARING VARIABLES

All variables must be declared prior to use. The general form of a declaration is

type variable_name;

For example, to declare **x** to be a **float**, **y** to be an integer, and **ch** to be a character, you would write

```
float x;
int y;
char ch;
```

You can declare more than one variable of a type by using a comma-separated list. For example, the following statement declares three integers:

```
int a, b, c;
```

Initializing Variables

A variable can be initialized by following its name with an equal sign and an initial value. For example, this declaration assigns **count** an initial value of 100:

```
int count = 100;
```

An initializer can be any expression that is valid when the variable is declared. This includes other variables and function calls. However, in C, global variables and **static** local variables must be initialized using only constant expressions.

IDENTIFIERS

Variable, function, and user-defined type names are all examples of *identifiers.* In C/C++ identifiers are sequences of letters, digits, and underscores from one to several characters in length. (A digit cannot begin an identifier, however.) Identifiers can be of any length, but, in C, only the first 31 characters are guaranteed to be significant. The underscore is often used for clarity, as in **first_time**, or to begin a name, as in **_count**. Uppercase and lowercase names are recognized as different. For example, **test** and **TEST** are two different variables. C++ reserves all identifiers that begin with two underscores or an underscore followed by an uppercase letter.

CLASSES

The *class* is C++'s basic unit of encapsulation. A class is defined using the **class** keyword. Classes are not part of the C language. A class is essentially a collection of variables and functions that manipulate those variables. The variables and functions that form a class are called *members.* The general form of **class** is shown here:

```
class class-name : inheritance-list {
  // private members by default
protected:
  // private members that may be inherited
public:
  // public members
} object-list;
```

Here, *class-name* is the name of the class type. Once the class declaration has been compiled, the *class-name* becomes a new data type name that can be used to declare objects of the class. The *object-list* is a comma-separated list of objects of type *class-name*. This list is optional. Class objects can be declared later in your program by simply using the class name. The *inheritance-list* is also optional. When present, it specifies the base class or classes that the new class inherits. (See the upcoming section entitled "Inheritance.")

A class can include a *constructor function* and a *destructor function*. (Both are optional.) A constructor is called when an object of the class is first created. The destructor is called when an object is destroyed. A constructor has the same name as the class. A destructor function has the same name as the class but is preceded by a ~ (tilde). Neither constructors nor destructors have return types. In a class hierarchy, constructors are executed in order of derivation and destructors are executed in reverse order.

By default, all elements of a class are private to that class and can only be accessed by other members of that class. To allow an element of the class to be accessed by functions that are not members of the class, you must declare them after the keyword **public**. For example,

```
class myclass {
  int a, b; // private to myclass
public:
  // class members accessible by nonmembers
  void setab(int i, int j) { a = i; b = j; }
  void showab() { cout << a << ' ' << b << endl; }
} ;

myclass ob1, ob2;
```

This declaration creates a class type, called **myclass**, that contains two private variables, **a** and **b**. It also contains two public functions called **setab()** and **showab()**. The fragment also declares two objects of type **myclass** called **ob1** and **ob2**.

To allow a member of a class to be inherited, but to otherwise be private, specify it as **protected**. A protected member is available to derived classes but is private within its class hierarchy.

When operating on an object of a class, use the dot (**.**) operator to reference individual members. The arrow operator (–>) is used when accessing an object through a pointer. For example, the following code listing accesses the **putinfo()** function of **ob** using the dot operator and the **show()** function using the arrow operator.

```
struct cl_type {
  int x;
  float f;
public:
  void putinfo(int a, float t) { x = a; f = t; }
  void show() { cout << a << ' ' << f << endl; }
} ;

cl_type ob, *p;

// ...

ob.putinfo(10, 0.23);

p = &ob; // put ob's address in p

p->show(); // displays ob's data
```

It is possible to create generic classes by using the **template** keyword. (See "**template**" in the "Keyword Summary.")

INHERITANCE

In C++, one class can inherit the characteristics of another. The inherited class is usually called the *base class.* The inheriting class is referred to as a *derived class.* When one class inherits another a *class hierarchy* is formed. The general form for inheriting a class is

class *class-name* : *access base-class-name* {
  // . . .
};

Here, *access* determines how the base class is inherited and it must be either **private**, **public**, or **protected**. (It can also be omitted, in which case **public** is assumed if the base class is a **struct**; or **private** if the base class is a **class**.) To inherit more than one class, use a comma-separated list.

If *access* is **public**, all **public** and **protected** members of the base class become **public** and **protected** members of the derived class, respectively. If *access* is **private**, all **public** and **protected** members of the base class become **private** members of the derived class. If *access* is **protected**, all **public** and **protected** members of the base class become **protected** members of the derived class.

In the following class hierarchy, **derived** inherits **base** as private. This means that **i** becomes a private member of **derived**.

```
class base {
public:
  int i;
};

class derived : private base {
  int j;
public:
  derived(int a) { j = i = a; }
  int getj() { return j; }
  int geti() { return i; } // OK, derived has access to i
};

derived ob(9); // create a derived object

cout << ob.geti() << " " << ob.getj(); // OK

// ob.i = 10; // ERROR, i is private to derived!
```

STRUCTURES

A structure is created using the keyword **struct**. In C++, a *structure* also defines a class. The only difference between **class** and **struct** is that by default, all members of a structure are public. To make a member private, you must use the **private** keyword. The general form of a structure declaration is this:

```
struct struct-name : inheritance-list{
  // public members by default
protected:
  // private members that may be inherited
private:
  // private members
} object-list;
```

In C, several restrictions apply to structures. First, they can contain only data members; member functions are not allowed. C structures do not support inheritance. Also, all members are public and the keywords **protected** and **private** cannot be used.

UNIONS

A *union* is a class type in which all data members share the same memory location. In C++, a union may include both member functions and data. All members of a union are public by default. To create private elements, you must use the **private** keyword. The general form for declaration of a **union** is

```
union class-name {
  // public members by default
private:
  // private members
} object-list;
```

In C, unions may contain only data members and the **private** keyword is not supported.

The elements of a union overlay each other. For example,

```
union tom {
  char ch;
  int x;
} t;
```

declares union **tom**, which looks like this in memory (assuming 2-byte integers):

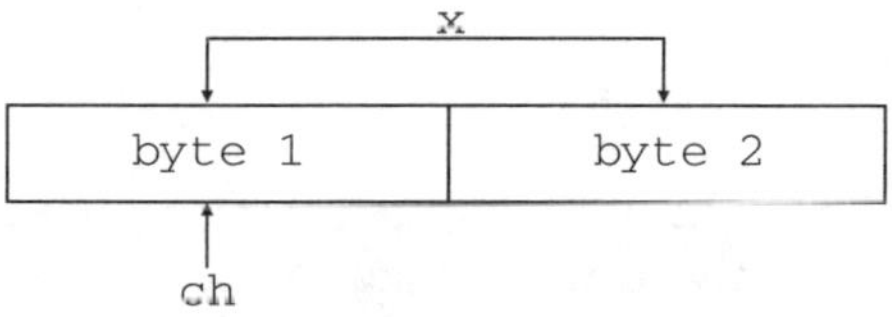

Like a class, the individual variables that compose the union are referenced using the dot operator. The arrow operator is used with a pointer to a union.

There are several restrictions that apply to unions. First, a union cannot inherit any other class of any type. A union cannot be a base class. A union cannot have virtual member functions. No members can be declared as static. A union cannot have as a member any object that overloads the = operator. Finally, no object can be a member of a union if the object's class explicitly defines a constructor or destructor function. (Objects that have only the default constructors and destructors are acceptable.)

There is a special type of union in C++ called an *anonymous union.* An anonymous union declaration does not contain a class name, and no objects of that union are declared. Instead, an anonymous union simply tells the compiler that its member variables are to share the same memory location. However, the variables themselves are referred to directly, without using the normal dot or arrow operator syntax. The variables that make up an anonymous union are at the same scope level as any other variable declared within the same block. This implies that the union variable names must not conflict with any other names that are valid within their scope. Here is an example of an anonymous union:

```
union { // anonymous union
  int a; // a and f share
  float f; // the same memory location
};

// ...

a = 10; // access a
cout << f; // access f
```

Here, **a** and **f** both share the same memory location. As you can see, the names of the union variables are referred to directly without the use of the dot or arrow operator.

All restrictions that apply to unions in general apply to anonymous unions. In addition, anonymous unions must contain only data—no member functions are allowed. Anonymous unions cannot contain the **private** or **protected** keywords. Finally, an anonymous union with namespace scope must be declared as **static**.

Programming Tip

In C++, it is common practice is to use **struct** when creating C-style structures that include only data members. A **class** is usually reserved for creating classes that contain function members. Sometimes the acronym *POD* is used to describe a C-style structure. POD stands for Plain Old Data.

ENUMERATIONS

Another type of variable that can be created is called an *enumeration*. An enumeration is a list of named integer constants. Thus, an enumeration type is simply a specification of the list of names that belong to the enumeration.

To create an enumeration requires the use of the keyword **enum**. The general form of an enumeration type is

enum *enum-name* { *list of names* } *var-list*;

The *enum-name* is the enumeration's type name. The list of names is comma-separated.

For example, the following fragment defines an enumeration of cities called **cities** and the variable **c** of type **cities**. Finally, **c** is assigned the value "Houston".

```
enum cities {Houston, Austin, Amarillo} c;
c = Houston;
```

In an enumeration, the value of the first (leftmost) name is, by default, 0; the second name has the value 1; the third has the value 2; and so on. In general, each name is given a value one greater than the name that precedes it. You can give a name a specific value by adding an initializer. For example, in the following enumeration, **Austin** will have the value 10.

```
enum cities {Houston, Austin=10, Amarillo };
```

In this example, **Amarillo** will have the value 11 because each name will be one greater than the one that precedes it.

In C++, an enumeration object can be assigned only those values defined by its enumeration type. In C, an enumeration object can be assigned any integer value.

C TAGS

In C, the name of a structure, union, or enumeration does not define a complete type name. In C++, it does. For example, the following fragment is valid for C++ but not for C.

```
struct s_type {
  int i;
  double d;
};
// ...
s_type x; // OK for C++, but not for C
```

In C++, **s_type** defines a complete type name and can be used, by itself, to declare objects. In C, **s_type** only defines a *tag*. In C, you need to precede a tag name with either **struct**, **union**, or **enum** when declaring objects. For example,

```
struct s_type x; // now OK for C
```

The preceding syntax is also permissible in C++, but it is seldom used.

THE STORAGE CLASS SPECIFIERS

The storage class specifiers **extern**, **auto**, **register**, **static**, and **mutable** are used to alter the way C/C++ creates storage for variables. These specifiers precede the type that they modify.

extern

If the **extern** specifier is placed before a variable name, the compiler will know that the variable has external linkage.

External linkage means that an object is visible outside its own file. In essence, **extern** tells the compiler the type of a variable without actually allocating storage for it. The **extern** modifier is most commonly used when there are two or more files sharing the same global variables.

auto

The specifier **auto** tells the compiler that the local variable it precedes is created upon entry into a block and destroyed upon exit from a block. Since all variables defined inside a function are **auto** by default, the **auto** keyword is seldom (if ever) used.

register

When C was first invented, **register** could only be used on local integer or character variables because it caused the compiler to attempt to keep that variable in a register of the CPU instead of placing it in memory. This made all references to that variable extremely fast. The definition of **register** has since been expanded. Now, any variable may be specified as **register** and it is the compiler's job to optimize accesses to it. For characters and integers, this still means putting them into a register in the CPU, but for other types of data, it may mean using cache memory, for example.

Keep in mind that **register** is only a request. The compiler is free to ignore it. The reason for this is that a limited number of variables can be optimized for speed. When this limit is exceeded, the compiler will simply ignore further **register** requests.

static

The **static** specifier instructs the compiler to keep a local variable in existence during the lifetime of the program instead of creating and destroying it each time it comes into and goes out of scope. Therefore, making local variables **static** allows them to maintain their values between function calls.

The **static** modifier can also be applied to global variables. When this is done, it causes that variable's scope to be restricted to the file in which it is declared. This means that it will have internal linkage. Internal linkage means that an identifier is known only within its own file.

In C++, when **static** is used on a class data member, it causes only one copy of that member to be shared by all objects of its class.

mutable

The **mutable** specifier applies to C++ only. It allows a member of an object to override **const**ness. That is, a **mutable** member of a **const** object is not **const** and may be modified.

TYPE QUALIFIERS

The type qualifiers **const** and **volatile** provide additional information about the variables they precede.

const

Objects of type **const** may not be changed by your program during execution. Also, an object pointed to by a **const** pointer cannot be modified. The compiler is free to place variables of this type into read-only memory (ROM). A **const** variable will receive its value either from an explicit initialization or by some hardware-dependent means. For example,

```
const int a = 10;
```

will create an integer called **a** with a value of 10 that may not be modified by your program. It can, however, be used in other types of expressions.

Programming Tip

If a class member function is modified by **const**, it cannot alter the object that invokes the function. To declare a **const** member function, put **const** after its parameter list. For example,

```
class MyClass {
  int i;
public:
  // a const function
  void wrong(int a) const {
    i = a; // Error! can't modify invoking object
  }
  void right(int a) {
    i = a; // OK, not const function
  }
};
```

As the comments suggest, **wrong()** is a **const** function, and it cannot modify the object that invokes it.

volatile

The modifier **volatile** tells the compiler that a variable's value may be changed in ways not explicitly specified by the program. For example, a global variable's address may be passed to the clock routine of the operating system and updated with each clock tick. In this situation, the contents of the variable are altered without any explicit assignment statements in the program. This is important because compilers sometimes automatically optimize certain expressions by making the assumption that the contents of a variable are unchanging inside an expression. This is done to achieve higher performance. The **volatile** modifier will prevent this optimization in those rare situations in which this assumption is not the case.

ARRAYS

You may declare arrays of any data type. The general form of a singly dimensioned array is

type var-name[*size*];

where *type* specifies the data type of each element in the array, and *size* specifies the number of elements in the array. For example, to declare an integer array **x** of 100 elements you would write

```
int x[100];
```

This will create an array that is 100 elements long with the first element being 0 and the last being 99. For example, the following loop will load the numbers 0 through 99 into array **x**.

```
for(t=0; t<100; t++) x[t] = t;
```

You can declare arrays of any valid data type, including classes that you create.

Multidimensional arrays are declared by placing the additional dimensions inside additional brackets. For example, to declare a 10 by 20 integer array you would write

```
int x[10][20];
```

Arrays can be initialized by using a bracketed list of initializers. For example,

```
int count[5] = { 1, 2, 3, 4, 5 };
```

DEFINING NEW TYPE NAMES USING typedef

You can create a new name for an existing type using **typedef**. Its general form is

typedef *type newname*;

For example, the following fragment of code tells the compiler that **feet** is another name for **int**:

```
typedef int feet;
```

Now, the following declaration is perfectly legal and creates an integer variable called distance.

```
feet distance;
```

CONSTANTS

Constants, also called *literals,* refer to fixed values that cannot be altered by the program. Constants can be of any of the basic data types. The way each constant is represented depends upon its type. Character constants are enclosed between single quotation marks. For example, 'a' and '+' are both character constants. Integer constants are specified as numbers without fractional components. For example, 10 and −100 are integer constants. Floating-point constants require the use of the decimal point followed by the number's fractional component. For example, 11.123 is a floating-point constant. You can also use scientific notation for floating-point numbers.

There are two floating-point types: **float** and **double**. Also, there are several flavors of the basic types that are generated using the type modifiers. By default, the compiler fits a numeric constant into the smallest compatible data type that will hold it. The only exceptions to the smallest type rule are floating-point constants, which are assumed to be of type **double**. For many programs, the compiler defaults are perfectly adequate. However, it is possible to specify precisely the type of constant you want.

To specify the exact type of numeric constant, use a suffix. For floating-point types, if you follow the number with an **F**, the number is treated as a **float**. If you follow it with an **L**, the number becomes a **long double**. For integer types, the **U** suffix stands for **unsigned** and the **L** for **long**. Some examples are shown here:

Data Type	**Constant Examples**
int	1 123 21000 −234
long int	35000L −34L
unsigned int	10000U 987U
float	123.23F 4.34e−3F
double	123.23 −0.9876324
long double	1001.2L

Hexadecimal and Octal Constants

It is sometimes easier to use a number system based on 8 or 16 instead of 10. The number system based on 8 is called *octal* and uses the digits 0 through 7. In octal the number 10 is the same as 8 in decimal. The base 16 number system is called *hexadecimal* and uses the digits 0 through 9 plus the letters A through F, which stand for 10, 11, 12, 13, 14, and 15. For example, the hexadecimal number 10 is 16 in decimal. Because of the frequency with which these two number systems are used, C/C++ allows you to specify integer constants in hexadecimal or octal instead of decimal if you prefer. A hexadecimal constant must begin with a 0x (a zero followed by an x) or 0X, followed by the constant in hexadecimal form. An octal constant begins with a zero. Here are two examples:

```
int hex = 0x80; // 128 in decimal
int oct = 012; // 10 in decimal
```

String Constants

C/C++ supports one other type of constant in addition to those of the predefined data types: a *string*. A string is a set of characters enclosed by double quotes. For example, "this is a test" is a string. You must not confuse strings with characters. A single character constant is enclosed by single quotes, such as 'a'. However, "a" is a string containing only one letter. String constants are automatically null terminated by the compiler. C++ also supports a **string** class, which is described later in this book.

Boolean Constants

C++ specifies two Boolean constants: **true** and **false**.

Backslash Character Constants

Enclosing character constants in single quotes works for most printing characters, but a few, such as the carriage return, are impossible to enter into your program's source code from the keyboard. For this reason, C/C++ recognizes several *backslash character constants*, also called *escape sequences*. These constants are listed here:

Code	**Meaning**
\b	Backspace
\f	Form feed
\n	Newline
\r	Carriage return

\t	Horizontal tab
\"	Double quote
\'	Single quote
\\	Backslash
\v	Vertical tab
\a	Alert
\N	Octal constant (where N is an octal constant)
\xN	Hexadecimal constant (where N is a hexadecimal constant)
\?	Question mark

The backslash constants can be used anywhere a character can. For example, the following statement outputs a newline and a tab and then prints the string, "This is a test":

```
cout << "\n\tThis is a test";
```

Chapter 2—Functions, Scopes, Namespaces, and Headers

Functions are the building blocks of a C/C++ program. The elements of a program, including functions, exist within one or more scopes. In C++, there is a special scope called a namespace. The prototypes for all standard functions are declared within various headers. These topics are examined here.

FUNCTIONS

At the heart of a C/C++ program is the function. It is the place in which all program activity occurs. The general form of a function is

ret-type function_name (parameter list)
{
  body of function
}

The type of data returned by a function is specified by *ret-type*. The *parameter list* is a comma-separated list of variables that will receive any arguments passed to the function. For example, the following function has two integer parameters called **i** and **j** and a **double** parameter called **count**:

```
void f(int i, int j, double count)
{ ...
```

Notice that you must declare each parameter separately.

In C++, if a function has no parameters, then its parameter list is empty. In C, to specify an empty parameter list, use the word **void**. Here is an example:

```
int f(void)
{ ...
```

This use of **void** in C++ is allowed but is redundant.

In C, if a function's return type is not explicitly specified, it defaults to integer. Standard C++ no longer supports "default-to-int," although most C++ compilers still allow it. Functions terminate and return automatically to the calling procedure when the last brace is encountered. You may force a return prior to that by using the **return** statement.

All functions, except those declared as **void**, return a value. The type of the return value must match the type declaration of the function. If a **return** statement is part of a non-**void** function, the return value of the function is the value in the **return** statement.

In C++, it is possible to create generic functions using the keyword **template**. (See "**template**" in the "Keyword Summary.")

RECURSION

In C/C++, functions can call themselves. This is called *recursion,* and a function that calls itself is said to be *recursive.* A simple example is the function **factr( )** shown here, which computes the factorial of an integer. The factorial of a number N is the product of all the whole numbers from 1 to N. For example, 3 factorial is 1 × 2 × 3, or 6.

```
// Compute the factorial of a number using recursion.
int factr(int n)
{
  int answer;

  if(n==1) return 1;
  answer = factr(n-1)*n;
  return answer;
}
```

When **factr( )** is called with an argument of 1, the function returns 1; otherwise it returns the product of **factr(n − 1) * n**. To evaluate this expression, **factr( )** is called with **n − 1**. This process continues until **n** equals 1 and the calls to the function begin returning. When **factr( )** finally returns to the original caller, the final return value will be the factorial of the original argument.

When a function calls itself, new local variables and parameters are allocated storage on the stack, and the function code is executed with these new variables from its beginning. A recursive call does not make a new copy of the function. Only the arguments are new. As each recursive call returns, the old local variables and parameters are removed from the stack and execution resumes at the point of the recursive call inside the function. Recursive functions could be said to "telescope" out and back.

Programming Tip

While powerful, recursive functions should be used with care. The recursive versions of many routines execute a bit more slowly than the iterative equivalent because of the added overhead of the repeated function calls. Many recursive calls to a function could cause a stack overrun. Because storage for function parameters and local variables is on the stack and each new call creates a new copy of these variables, the stack space could become exhausted. If this happens, a *stack overflow* occurs. If this occurs in the normal use of a debugged recursive function, try increasing the stack space allocated to your program.

When writing recursive functions, you must include a conditional statement somewhere that causes the function to return without the recursive call being executed. If you don't, once you call the function, it will call itself until the stack is exhausted. This is a very common error when developing recursive functions. Use output statements liberally during development so that you can watch what is going on and abort execution if you see that you have made a mistake.

FUNCTION OVERLOADING

In C++, functions may be *overloaded.* When a function is overloaded, two or more functions share the same name. However, each version of an overloaded function must have a different number or type of parameters. (The function return types may also differ, but this is not necessary.) When an overloaded function is called, the compiler decides which version of the function to use based upon the type and number of arguments, calling the function that has the closest match. For example, given these three overloaded functions,

```
void myfunc(int a) {
  cout << "a is " << a << endl;
}

// overload myfunc
void myfunc(int a, int b) {
  cout << "a is " << a << endl;
  cout << "b is " << b << endl;
}
```

```
// overload myfunc, again
void myfunc(int a, double b) {
  cout << "a is " << a << endl;
  cout << "b is " << b << endl;
}
```

the following calls are allowed:

```
myfunc(10); // calls myfunc(int)
myfunc(12, 24); // calls myfunc(int, int)
myfunc(99, 123.23); // calls myfunc(int, double)
```

In each case, the type and number of arguments determine which version of **myfunc( )** is actually executed.

Function overloading is not supported by C.

DEFAULT ARGUMENTS

In C++ you may assign a function parameter a default value, which will be used automatically when no corresponding argument is specified when the function is called. The default value is specified in a manner syntactically similar to a variable initialization. For example, this function assigns its two parameters default values:

```
void myfunc(int a = 0, int b = 10)
{ // ...
```

Given the default arguments, **myfunc( )** can be legally called in these three ways:

```
myfunc(~); // a defaults to 0; b defaults to 10
myfunc(-1); // a is passed -1; b defaults to 10
myfunc(-1, 99); // a is passed -1; b is 99
```

When you create functions that have default arguments, you must specify the default values only once, either in the function prototype or in its definition. (You cannot specify them each place, even if you use the same values.) Generally, default values are specified in the prototype.

When giving a function default arguments remember that you must specify all nondefaulting arguments first. Once you begin to specify default arguments, there may be no intervening nondefaulting ones.

Default arguments are not supported by C.

PROTOTYPES

In C++, all functions must be prototyped. In C, prototypes are technically optional but strongly recommended. The general form of a prototype is shown here:

ret-type name(*parameter list*);

In essence, a *prototype* is simply the return type, name, and parameter list of a function's definition, followed by a semicolon.

The following example shows how the function **fn( )** is prototyped:

```
float fn(float x); // prototype

   .
   .
   .
// function definition
float fn(float x)
{
  // ...
}
```

To specify the prototype for a function that takes a variable number of arguments, use three periods at the point at which the variable number of parameters begins. For example, the **printf( )** function could be prototyped like this:

```
int printf(const char *format, ...);
```

When specifying the prototype to an overloaded function, each version of that function must have its own prototype. When a member function is declared within its class, this constitutes a prototype for the function.

In C, to specify the prototype for a function that has no parameters, use **void** in its parameter list.

Programming Tip

Two terms are commonly confused in C/C++ programming: *declaration* and *definition*. Here is what they mean. A declaration specifies the name and type of an object. A definition allocates storage for it. These meanings apply to functions, too. A function declaration (prototype) specifies the return type, name, and parameters of a function. The function itself (that is, the function with its body) is its definition.

In many cases, a declaration is also a definition. For example, when a non-**extern** variable is declared, it is also defined. Or, when a function is defined prior to its first use, its definition also serves as its declaration.

UNDERSTANDING SCOPES AND VARIABLE LIFETIMES

C and C++ define *scope rules,* which govern the visibility and lifetime of objects. Although there are several subtleties, in the most general sense, there are two scopes: *global* and *local.*

The global scope exists outside all other scopes. A name declared in the global scope is known throughout the program. For example, a global variable is available for use by all functions in the program. Global variables stay in existence the entire duration of the program.

A local scope is defined by a block. That is, a local scope is begun by an opening brace and ends with its closing brace. A name declared within a local scope is known only within that scope. Because blocks can be nested, local scopes, too, can be nested. Of course the most common local scope is the one defined by a function. Local variables are created when their block is entered and destroyed when their block is exited. This means that local variables do not hold their values between function calls. You can use the **static** modifier, however, to preserve values between calls.

In C++, local variables may be declared nearly anywhere within a block. In C, they must be declared at the start of a block, before any "action" statements occur. For example, the following code is valid for C++, but not for C:

```
void f(int a)
{
  int a;

  a = 10;

  int b; // OK for C++, but not C
```

A global variable must be declared outside of all functions, including the **main( )** function. Global variables are generally placed at the top of the file, prior to **main( )**, for ease of reading and because a variable must be declared before it is used.

The formal parameters to a function are also local variables and, aside from their job of receiving the value of the calling arguments, behave and can be used like any other local variable.

NAMESPACES

In C++ it is possible to create a local scope using the **namespace** keyword. A namespace defines a declarative region. Its purpose is to localize names. The general form of **namespace** is shown here:

```
namespace name {
  // . . .
}
```

Here, *name* is the name of the namespace. Here is an example:

```
namespace MyNameSpace {
  int count;
}
```

This creates a namespace called **MyNameSpace** and the variable **count** is declared inside it.

Names declared within a namespace can be referred to directly by other statements within the same namespace. Outside their namespace, names can be accessed two ways. First, you can use the scope resolution operator. For example, assuming **MyNameSpace** just shown, the following statement is valid:

```
MyNameSpace::count = 10;
```

You can also specify a **using** statement, which brings the specified name or namespace into the current scope. Here is an example:

```
using namespace MyNameSpace;
count = 100;
```

In this case, **count** can be referred to directly because it has been brought into the current scope.

Traditionally, items declared in the C++ library were in the global (i.e., unnamed) namespace. However, the current specification for C++ puts all of these items into the **std** namespace.

THE main( ) FUNCTION

In C/C++ program, execution begins at **main( )**. (Windows programs call **WinMain( )**, but this is a special case.) You must not have more than one function called **main( )**. When **main( )** terminates, the program is over and control passes back to the operating system.

The **main( )** function is not prototyped. Thus, different forms of **main( )** may be used. For both C and C++, the following versions of **main( )** are valid. (Other forms are also allowed.)

```
int main()
int main(int argc, char *argv[])
```

As the second form shows, at least two parameters are supported by **main( )**. They are **argc** and **argv**. (Some compilers will allow additional parameters.) These two variables will hold the number of command-line arguments and a pointer to them, respectively. The parameter **argc** is an integer, and its value will always be at least 1 because the program name is the first argument as far as C/C++ is concerned. The parameter **argv** must be declared as an array of character pointers. Each pointer points to a command-line argument. Their usage is shown below in a short program that will print your name on the screen:

```
#include <iostream>
using namespace std;

int main(int argc, char *argv[])
{
  if(argc<2)
    cout << "Enter your name.\n";
  else
    cout << "hello " << argv[1];

  return 0;
}
```

FUNCTION ARGUMENTS

If a function is to use arguments, it must declare variables that accept the values of the arguments. These variables are called the *formal parameters* of the function. They behave like other local variables inside the function and are created upon entry into the function and destroyed upon exit. As with local variables, you can make assignments to a function's formal parameters or use them in any allowable C/C++ expression. Even though these variables perform the special task of receiving the value of the arguments passed to the function, they can be used like any other local variable.

In general, subroutines can be passed arguments in one of two ways. The first is called *call by value.* This method copies the value of an argument into the formal parameter of the subroutine. Changes made to the parameters of the subroutine have no effect on the variables used to call it. The second way a subroutine can have arguments passed to it is by means of a *call by reference.* In this method, the *address* of an argument is copied into the parameter. Inside the subroutine, the address is used to access the actual argument used in the call. This means that changes made to the parameter affect the variable used to call the routine.

By default, C and C++ use call by value to pass arguments. This means that within a function you generally cannot alter the variables used to call the function. Consider the following function:

```
int sqr(int x)
{
  x = x*x;
  return x;
}
```

In this example, when the assignment **x** = **x** * **x** takes place, the only thing modified is the local variable **x**. The argument used to call **sqr( )** still has its original value.

Remember that only a copy of the value of the argument is passed to a function. What occurs inside the function has no effect on the variable used in the call.

Passing Pointers

Even though C and C++ use call by value parameter-passing by default, it is possible to manually construct a call by reference by passing a pointer to the argument. Since this passes the address of the argument to the function, it is then possible to change the value of the argument outside the function.

Pointers are passed to functions just like any other value. Of course, it is necessary to declare the parameters as pointer types. For example, the function **swap( )**, which exchanges the value of its two integer arguments, follows:

```
// Use pointer parameters.
void swap(int *x, int *y)
{
  int temp;

  temp = *x; // save the value at address x
  *x = *y; // put y into x
  *y = temp; // put x into y
}
```

It is important to remember that **swap( )** (or any other function that uses pointer parameters) must be called with the *addresses of the arguments.* The following fragment shows the correct way to call **swap( )**:

```
int a, b;

a = 10;
b = 20;
swap(&a, &b);
```

In this example, **swap( )** is called with the addresses of **a** and **b**. The unary operator **&** is used to produce the addresses of the variables. Therefore, the addresses of **a** and **b**, not their values, are passed to the function **swap( )**. After the call, **a** will have the value 20 and **b** will have the value 10.

Reference Parameters

In C++ it is possible to automatically pass the address of a variable to a function. This is accomplished using a *reference parameter.* When using a reference parameter, the address of an argument is passed to the function and the function operates on the argument, not a copy.

To create a reference parameter, precede its name with the **&** (ampersand). Inside the function, you may use the parameter normally, without any need to use the * (asterisk) operator. The compiler will automatically dereference the address for you. For example, the following code creates a version of **swap( )** that uses two reference parameters to exchange the values of its two arguments:

```
// Use reference parameters.
void swap(int &x, int &y)
{
  int temp;

  temp = x; // save the value at address x
  x = y; // put y into x
  y = temp; // put x into y
}
```

When invoking **swap( )**, you simply use the normal function-call syntax. Here is an example:

```
int a, b;

a = 10;
b = 20;
swap(a, b);
```

Because **x** and **y** are now reference parameters, the addresses of **a** and **b** are automatically generated and passed to the function. Inside the function, the parameter names are used without any need for the * operator because the compiler automatically refers to the calling arguments each time **x** and **y** are used.

Reference parameters only apply to C++.

CONSTRUCTORS AND DESTRUCTORS

In C++, a class may contain a constructor function, a destructor function, or both. A constructor is called when an object of the class is first created and the destructor is called when an object of the class is destroyed. A constructor has the same name as the class of which it is a member, and the destructor's name is the same as its class, except that it is preceded by a ~ (tilde). Neither constructors nor destructors have return values.

Constructor functions may have parameters. You can use these parameters to pass values to a constructor function, which can be used to initialize an object. The arguments that are passed to the parameters are specified when each object is created. For example, this fragment illustrates how to pass a constructor an argument:

```
class myclass {
  int a;
public:
  myclass(int i) { a = i; } // constructor
  ~myclass() { cout << "Destructing..."; }
};

// ...

myclass ob(3); // pass 3 to i
```

When **ob** is declared, the value 3 is passed to the constructor's parameter **i**, which is then assigned to **a**.

FUNCTION SPECIFIERS

C++ defines three function specifiers: **inline**, **virtual**, and **explicit**. The specifier **inline** is a request to the compiler to expand a function's code in line rather than to call it. If the compiler cannot inline the function, it is free to ignore the request. Both member and nonmember functions may be specified as **inline**.

A **virtual** function is defined in a base class and overridden by a derived class. Virtual functions are how C++ supports polymorphism.

The **explicit** specifier applies only to constructors. A constructor specified as **explicit** will only be used when an initialization exactly matches that specified by the constructor. No automatic conversion will take place. (It creates a "nonconverting constructor.")

LINKAGE SPECIFICATION

Because it is common to link a C++ function with functions generated by another language (such as C), C++ allows you to specify a *linkage specification* that tells the compiler how to link a function. It has this general form:

extern "*language*" *function-prototype*

As you can see, the linkage specification is an extension to the **extern** keyword. Here, *language* denotes the language to which you want the function to link. C and C++ linkage are guaranteed to be supported. Your compiler may support other linkages, too. To declare several functions using the same linkage specification, you can use this general form:

extern "*language*" {
  function-prototypes
}

The linkage specification applies only to C++. It is not supported by C.

THE C AND C++ STANDARD LIBRARIES

Neither C nor C++ has keywords that perform I/O, manipulate strings, perform various mathematical computations, or carry out a number of other useful procedures. The way these things are accomplished is by using a set of predefined library functions that are supplied with the compiler. There are two basic styles of libraries: the C function library, which is supplied with all C and C++ compilers, and the C++ class library, which applies only to C++. Both libraries are summarized later in this guide.

Before your program can use a library function, it must include the appropriate *header.* For C programs, headers are specified using their file names, which end in .H. The header files that are defined by the ANSI C standard are shown here:

C Header File	**Supports**
assert.h	The **assert( )** macro
ctype.h	Character handling
errno.h	Error reporting
float.h	Implementation-dependent floating-point values
iso646.h	Several macros that can be used in place of various operators, such as **not** for ! or **xor** for ^
limits.h	Various implementation-dependent limits
locale.h	The **setlocale( )** function
math.h	Various definitions used by the math library
setjmp.h	Nonlocal jumps
signal.h	Signal values
stdarg.h	Variable-length argument lists
stddef.h	Commonly used constants
stdio.h	File I/O

C Header File	Supports
stdlib.h	Miscellaneous declarations
string.h	String functions
time.h	System time and date functions
wctype.h	Wide character handling
wchar.h	Wide character-enabled functions

In the modern specification for C++, headers are specified using standard header names, which do not end with .h. These new-style C++ headers do not specify file names. Instead, they are simply standard identifiers that the compiler can handle as it sees fit. This means that a header may be mapped to a file name, but this is not required. The new-style C++ headers are shown here. Those associated with the Standard Template Library (STL) are indicated.

C++ Header	Supports
<algorithm>	Various operations on containers (STL)
<bitset>	Bitsets (STL)
<complex>	Complex numbers
<deque>	Double-ended queues (STL)
<exception>	Exception handling
<fstream>	Stream-based file I/O
<functional>	Various functions (STL)
<iomanip>	I/O manipulators
<ios>	Low-level I/O classes
<iosfwd>	Forward declarations for I/O system
<iostream>	Standard I/O classes
<istream>	Input streams
<iterator>	Access to contents of containers (STL)
<limits>	Various implementation limits
<list>	Linear lists (STL)
<locale>	Localization specific information

C++ Header	Supports
<map>	Maps (keys with values) (STL)
<memory>	Memory allocation (STL)
<new>	Memory allocation using **new**
<numeric>	General-purpose numeric operations
<ostream>	Output streams
<queue>	Queues (STL)
<set>	Sets (STL)
<sstream>	String streams
<stack>	Stacks (STL)
<stdexcept>	Standard exceptions
<streambuf>	Buffered streams
<string>	Standard **string** class (STL)
<typeinfo>	Runtime type information
<utility>	General purpose templates (STL)
<valarray>	Operations on arrays containing values
<vector>	Vectors (dynamic arrays) (STL)

C++ also defines the following new-style headers that correspond to the C headers:

<cassert>	<cctype>	<cerrno>
<cfloat>	<ciso646>	<climits>
<clocale>	<cmath>	<csetjmp>
<csignal>	<cstdarg>	<cstddef>
<cstdio>	<cstdlib>	<cstring>
<ctime>	<cwchar>	<cwctype>

In standard C++, all of the information relating to the standard library is defined under the **std** namespace. Thus, to gain direct access to these items, you will need to include the following **using** statement after including the necessary headers.

```
using namespace std;
```

Programming Tip

If you are using an older C++ compiler, then it may not support the new-style C++ headers or the **namespace** command. If this is the case, then you will need to use the older, traditional-style headers. These use the same names as the new headers but include the .h. (Thus, they resemble C headers.) For example, the following includes < **iostream** > using the traditional approach:

```
#include <iostream.h>
```

When using the traditional-style header, all of the names defined by the header are placed in the global namespace, not the one defined by **std.** Thus, no **using** statement is required.

Chapter 3—Operators

C/C++ has a rich set of operators that can be divided into the following classes: arithmetic, relational and logical, bitwise, pointer, assignment, I/O, and miscellaneous.

ARITHMETIC OPERATORS

C/C++ has the following seven arithmetic operators:

Operator	**Action**
–	Subtraction, unary minus
+	Addition
*	Multiplication
/	Division
%	Modulus
––	Decrement
++	Increment

The +, –, *, and / operators work in the expected fashion. The % operator returns the remainder of an integer division. The increment and decrement operators increase or decrease the operand by one.

These operators have the following order of precedence:

Precedence	**Operators**
Highest	++ –– – (unary minus)
	* / %
Lowest	+ –

Operators on the same precedence level are evaluated left to right.

RELATIONAL AND LOGICAL OPERATORS

The relational and logical operators are used to produce true/false results and are often used together. In C/C++, *any* nonzero number evaluates as true. Zero is false. In C++, the outcome of the relational and logical operators is of type **bool**. In C, the outcome is a zero or nonzero integer. The relational operators are listed here:

Operator	Meaning
>	Greater than
>=	Greater than or equal to
<	Less than
<=	Less than or equal to
==	Equal to
!=	Not equal to

The logical operators are shown here:

Operator	Meaning
&&	AND
||	OR
!	NOT

The relational operators are used to compare two values. The logical operators are used to connect two values or, in the case of **!**, to reverse a value. The precedence of these operators is shown in the following table.

Precedence	Operators
Highest	!
	> >= < <=
	== !=
	&&
Lowest	||

As an example, the following **if** statement evaluates to true and prints the line **x is less than 10**:

```
x = 9;
if(x < 10) cout << "x is less than 10";
```

However, in the following example, no message is displayed because both operands associated with **&&** must be true for the outcome to be true.

```
x = 9;
y = 9;
if(x < 10 && y > 10)
  cout << "This will not print.";
```

THE BITWISE OPERATORS

C and C++ provide operators that act upon the actual bits that comprise a value. The bitwise operators can only be used on integral types. The bitwise operators are

Operator	Meaning
&	AND
|	OR
^	XOR
~	One's complement
>>	Right shift
<<	Left shift

&, |, and ^

The truth tables for **&**, |, and ^ are

p	q	p & q	p | q	p ^ q
0	0	0	0	0
0	1	0	1	1
1	1	1	1	0
1	0	0	1	1

These rules are applied to each bit in each operand when the bitwise AND, OR, and XOR operations are performed.

For example, a sample bitwise AND operation is shown here:

```
  0 1 0 0 1 1 0 1
& 0 0 1 1 1 0 1 1
  ---------------
  0 0 0 0 1 0 0 1
```

A bitwise OR operation looks like this:

```
  0 1 0 0 1 1 0 1
| 0 0 1 1 1 0 1 1
  ---------------
  0 1 1 1 1 1 1 1
```

A bitwise XOR operation is shown here:

```
  0 1 0 0 1 1 0 1
^ 0 0 1 1 1 0 1 1
  ---------------
  0 1 1 1 0 1 1 0
```

The One's Complement Operator

The one's complement operator, ~, will invert all the bits in its operand. For example, if a character variable, **ch**, has the bit pattern

```
0 0 1 1 1 0 0 1
```

then

```
ch = ~ch;
```

places the bit pattern

```
1 1 0 0 0 1 1 0
```

into **ch**.

The Shift Operators

The right (>>) and left (<<) shift operators shift all bits in an integral value by the specified amount. As bits are shifted off one end, zeros are brought in the other end. (If the value being shifted is a negative, signed number and a right shift is performed, then ones are shifted in to preserve the sign.) The number on the right side of the shift operator specifies the number of positions to shift. The general form of each shift operator is

value >> *number*
value << *number*

Here, *number* specifies the number of positions to shift *value.*

Given the bit pattern (and assuming an unsigned value)

```
0 0 1 1 1 1 0 1
```

a shift right yields

```
0 0 0 1 1 1 1 0
```

and a shift left produces

```
0 1 1 1 1 0 1 0
```

Programming Tip

A shift right is effectively a division by 2, and a shift left is a multiplication by 2. For many computers, a shift is faster than a multiply or a divide. Therefore, if you need a fast way to multiply or divide by 2, consider using the shift operators. For example, the following code fragment will first multiply and then divide the value in **x** by 2.

```
int x;

x = 10;
x = x << 1;
x = x >> 1;
```

Of course, when using the shift operators to perform multiplication, you must be careful not to shift bits off the end.

The precedence of the bitwise operators is shown here:

<table>
<tr><th>Precedence</th><th>Operators</th></tr>
<tr><td>Highest</td><td>~</td></tr>
<tr><td></td><td>>> <<</td></tr>
<tr><td></td><td>&</td></tr>
<tr><td></td><td>^</td></tr>
<tr><td>Lowest</td><td>|</td></tr>
</table>

POINTER OPERATORS

The two pointer operators are * and **&**. A *pointer* is a variable that contains the address of another object. Or, put differently, a variable that contains the address of another object is said to "point to" the other object.

The & Pointer Operator

The **&** operator returns the address of the object it precedes. For example, if the integer **x** is located at memory address 1000, then

```
p = &x;
```

places the value 1000 into **p**. The **&** can be thought of as "the address of." For example, the previous statement could be read as "place the address of **x** into **p**."

The * Pointer Operator

The * is the *indirection operator.* It uses the current value of the variable it precedes as the address at which data will be stored or obtained. For example, the fragment

```
p = &x; /* put address of x into p */
*p = 100; /* use address contained in p */
```

places the value 100 into **x**. The * can be remembered as "at address." In this example, the second line could be read, "place the value 100 at address **p**." Since **p** contains the address of **x**, the value 100 is actually stored in **x**. In words, **p** is said to "point to" **x**. The * operator can also be used on the right-hand side of an assignment. For example,

```
p = &x;
*p = 100;
z = *p/10;
```

places the value 10 into **z**.

ASSIGNMENT OPERATORS

In C/C++, the assignment operator is the single equal sign. When assigning a common value to several values, you can "string together" several assignments. For example,

```
a = b = c = 10;
```

assigns **a**, **b**, and **c** the value 10.

C/C++ allows a convenient form of "shorthand" for assignments of this general form:

var = var op expression;

Assignments of this type can be shortened to

var op = expression;

For example, the two assignments

```
x = x+10;
y = y/z;
```

can be recoded as shown here:

```
x += 10;
y /= z;
```

THE ? OPERATOR

The **?** operator is a *ternary operator* (it works on three operands). It has this general form:

expression1 ? expression2 : expression3;

If *expression1* is true, then the outcome of the operation is *expression2;* otherwise it is the value of *expression3.*

Programming Tip

The **?** is often used to replace **if-else** statements of this general type:

if(*expression1*) *var* = *expression2*;
else *var* = *expression3*;

For example, the sequence

```
if(y < 10) x = 20;
else x = 40;
```

can be rewritten like this:

```
x = (y<10) ? 20 : 40;
```

Here, **x** is assigned the value of 20 if **y** is less than 10 and 40 if it is not.

One reason that the **?** operator exists, beyond saving typing on your part, is that the compiler can produce very fast code for this statement—much faster than for the similar **if-else** statements.

MEMBER OPERATORS

The **.** (dot) operator and the −> (arrow) operator are used to reference individual members of classes, structures, and unions. The dot operator is applied to the actual object. The arrow operator is used with a pointer to an object. For example, given the following structure,

```
struct date_time {
  char date[16];
  int time;
} tm;
```

to assign the value "3/12/99" to the **date** member of object **tm**, you would write

```
strcpy(tm.date, "3/12/99");
```

However, if **p_tm** is a pointer to an object of type **date_time**, the following statement is used:

```
strcpy(p_tm->date, "3/12/99");
```

THE COMMA OPERATOR

The comma operator causes a sequence of operations to be performed. The value of the entire comma expression is the value of the last expression of the comma-separated list. For example, after execution of the following fragment,

```
y = 15;
x = (y=y-5, 50/y);
```

x will have the value 5 because **y**'s original value of 15 is reduced by 5 and then that value is divided into 50, yielding 5 as the result. You can think of the comma operator as meaning "do this and this" and so on.

The comma operator is used most often in the **for** statement. For example,

```
for(z=10, b=20; z<b; z++, b--) { // ...
```

Here, **z** and **b** are initialized and modified using comma-separated expressions.

sizeof

Although **sizeof** is also a keyword, it is a compile-time operator used to determine the size, in bytes, of a variable or data type, including classes, structures, and unions. If used with a type, the type name must be enclosed by parentheses.

For most 32-bit compilers, the following example prints the number 4:

```
int x;
cout << sizeof x;
```

THE CAST

A *cast* is a special operator that forces one data type to be converted into another. Both C and C++ support the form of cast shown here:

(*type*) *expression*

where *type* is the desired data type.

For example, the following cast causes the outcome of the specified integer division to be of type **double**:

```
double d;
d = (double) 10/3;
```

C++ Casts

C++ supports additional casting operators. They are **const_cast**, **dynamic_cast**, **reinterpret_cast**, and **static_cast**. Their general forms are

const_cast<*type*> (*object*)

dynamic_cast<*type*> (*object*)

reinterpret_cast<*type*> (*object*)

static_cast<*type*> (*object*)

Here, *type* specifies the target type of the cast and *object* is the object being cast into the new type.

The **const_cast** operator is used to explicitly override **const** and/or **volatile** in a cast. The target type must be the same as the source type except for the alteration of its **const** or **volatile** attributes. The most common use of **const_cast** is to remove **const**-ness.

The operator **dynamic_cast** performs a runtime cast that verifies the validity of the cast. If the cast cannot be made, the cast fails and the expression evaluates to null. Its main use is for performing casts on polymorphic types. For example, given two polymorphic classes B and D, with D derived from B, a **dynamic_cast** can always cast a D* pointer into a B* pointer. A **dynamic_cast** can cast a B* pointer into a D* pointer only if the object being pointed to actually is a D*. In general, **dynamic_cast** will succeed if the attempted polymorphic cast is permitted (that is, if the target type can legally apply to the type of object being cast). If the cast cannot be made, then **dynamic_cast** evaluates to null.

The **static_cast** operator performs a nonpolymorphic cast. For example, it can be used to cast a base class pointer into a derived class pointer. It can also be used for any standard conversion. No runtime checks are performed The **reinterpret_cast** operator changes one type into a fundamentally different type. For example, it can be used to change a pointer into an integer. A **reinterpret_cast** should be used for casting inherently incompatible pointer types.

Only **const_cast** can cast away **const**-ness. That is, neither **dynamic_cast**, **static_cast**, nor **reinterpret_cast** can alter the **const**-ness of an object.

THE I/O OPERATORS

In C++, the << and the >> are overloaded to perform I/O operations. When used in an expression in which the left operand is a stream, the >> is an input operator, and the << is an output operator. In the language of C++, the >> is called an *extractor* because it extracts data from the input stream. The << is called an *inserter* because it inserts data into the output stream. The general forms of these operators are

input-stream >> *variable*

output-stream << *expression*

For example, the following fragment inputs two integer variables:

```
int i, j;
cin >> i >> j;
```

The following statement displays "This is a test 10 20":

```
cout << "This is a test " << 10 << ' ' << 4*5;
```

The I/O operators are not supported by C.

THE .* AND ->* POINTER TO MEMBER OPERATORS

C++ allows you to generate a special type of pointer that "points" generically to a member of a class, not to a specific instance of that member in an object. This sort of pointer is called a *pointer to a member.* A pointer to a member is not the same as a normal C++ pointer. Instead, a pointer to a member provides only an offset into an object of the member's class at which that member can be found. Since member pointers are not true pointers, the **.** and **->** operators cannot be applied to them. To access a member of a class given a pointer to it, you must use the special pointer-to-member operators **.*** and **->***.

When you are accessing a member of an object given an object or a reference to an object, use the **.*** operator. When accessing a member given a pointer to an object, use the **->*** operator.

A pointer to a member is declared by using the general form shown here:

type class-name::**ptr*;

Here, *type* is the base type of the member, *class-name* is the name of the class, and *ptr* is the name of the pointer-to-member variable being created. Once created, *ptr* can point to any member of its class that is of type *type.*

Here is a short example that demonstrates the **.*** operator. Pay special attention to the way the member pointers are declared.

```
#include <iostream>
using namespace std;

class cl {
public:
  cl(int i) { val=i; }
  int val;
  int double_val() { return val+val; }
};
```

```
int main()
{
  int cl::*data; // int data member pointer
  int (cl::*func)(); // func member pointer
  cl ob1(1), ob2(2); // create objects

  data = &cl::val; // get offset
  func = &cl::double_val; // get offset

  cout << "Here are values: ";
  cout << ob1.*data << " " << ob2.*data << "\n";

  cout << "Here they are doubled: ";
  cout << (ob1.*func)() << " ";
  cout << (ob2.*func)() << "\n";

  return 0;
}
```

The pointer-to-member operators are not supported by C.

THE :: SCOPE RESOLUTION OPERATOR

The **::** *scope resolution operator* specifies the scope to which a member belongs. It has this general form:

name::*member-name*

Here, *name* is the name of the class or namespace that contains the member specified by *member-name.* Put differently, *name* specifies the scope within which can be found the identifier specified by *member-name.*

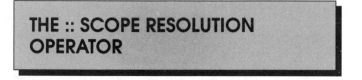

To reference the global scope, you do not specify a scope name. For example, to refer to a global variable called **count** that is being hidden by a local variable called **count**, you can use this statement.

```
::count
```

The scope resolution operator is not supported by C.

new AND delete

The operators **new** and **delete** are C++'s dynamic allocation operators. They are also keywords. See Chapter 5 for details.

C does not support the **new** and **delete** operators.

typeid

In C++, the **typeid** operator returns a reference to a **type_info** object that describes the type of the object to which **typeid** is being applied. The general form of **typeid** is

typeid(object)

The operator **typeid** supports runtime type identification (RTTI) in C++.

The **type_info** class defines the following public members:

bool operator==(const type_info &ob) const;

bool operator!=(const type_info &ob) const;

bool before(const type_info &ob) const;

const char *name( ) const;

The overloaded == and != provide for the comparison of types. The **before( )** function returns true if the invoking object is before the object used as a parameter in collation order. (This function is mostly for internal use. Its return value has nothing to do with inheritance or class hierarchies.) The **name( )** function returns a pointer to the name of the type.

When **typeid** is applied to a base class pointer of a polymorphic class, it will automatically return the type of the object being pointed to. (A polymorphic class is one that contains at least one virtual function.) Thus, **typeid** can be used to determine the type of object pointed to by a base class pointer.

C does not support **typeid**.

OPERATOR OVERLOADING

In C++, operators may be overloaded by using the **operator** keyword. (See Chapter 5.) Operator overloading is not supported by C.

OPERATOR PRECEDENCE SUMMARY

The following table lists the precedence of all C and C++ operators. Please note that all operators, except the unary operators, the assignment operators, and **?**, associate from left to right.

Precedence	**Operators**
Highest	( ) [ ] -> :: .
	! ~ ++ -- - * & sizeof new delete typeid *type-casts*
	.* ->*
	* / %
	+ -
	<< >>
	< <= > >=
	== !=
	&
	^
	|
	&&
	||
	?:
	= += -= *= /= %= >>= <<= &= ^= |=
Lowest	,

Chapter 4—The Preprocessor and Comments

C and C++ include several preprocessor directives, which are used to give instructions to the compiler. The preprocessor directives are listed here:

#define	#error	#include
#elif	#if	#line
#else	#ifdef	#pragma
#endif	#ifndef	#undef

Each is discussed briefly in this section.

#define

The directive **#define** is used to perform macro substitutions of one piece of text for another throughout the file in which it is used. The general form of the directive is

#define *macro-name character-sequence*

Here, each time *macro-name* is encountered the specified *character-sequence* is substituted. Notice that there is no semicolon in this statement. Furthermore, once the character sequence has started, it is terminated only by the end of the line.

For example, if you wish to use the value 1 for the word "TRUE" and the value 0 for the word "FALSE", you would declare these two macro **#define** statements:

```
#define TRUE 1
#define FALSE 0
```

This will cause the compiler to substitute a 1 or a 0 each time the word TRUE or FALSE is encountered.

The **#define** directive has another feature: The macro can have arguments. A macro that takes arguments acts much like a function. In fact, this type of macro is often referred to as a *function-like macro.* Each time the macro is encountered, the arguments associated with it are replaced by the actual arguments found in the program. Here is an example:

```
#include <iostream>
using namespace std;

#define ABS(a)  ((a)<0 ? -(a) : (a))

int main()
{
  cout << "abs of -1 and 1: " << ABS(-1)
       << ' ' << ABS(1);

  return 0;
}
```

When this program is compiled, **a** in the macro definition will be substituted with the values −1 and 1.

Programming Tip

You must be sure to completely parenthesize function-like macros that you create. If you don't, they may not work in all situations. For example, the parentheses surrounding **a** in the preceding example are necessary to ensure proper substitution in all cases. If the parentheses around **a** were removed, the expression

```
ABS(10-20)
```

would be converted to

```
10-20<0 ? -10-20 : 10-20
```

thus yielding the wrong result. If you have a function-like macro that misbehaves, check your parentheses.

#error

The **#error** directive forces the compiler to stop compilation when it is encountered. It is used primarily for debugging. Its general form is

#error *message*

When **#error** is encountered, the message and the line number are displayed.

#if, #ifdef, #ifndef, #else, #elif, AND #endif

The **#if**, **#ifdef**, **#ifndef**, **#else**, **#elif**, and **#endif** preprocessor directives are used to selectively compile various portions of a program. The general idea is that if the expression after an **#if**, **#ifdef**, or **#ifndef** is true, the code that is between one of the preceding and an **#endif** will be compiled; otherwise it will be skipped over. The **#endif** is used to mark the end of an **#if** block. The **#else** can be used with any of the above to provide an alternative.

The general form of **#if** is

#if *constant-expression*

If the constant expression is true, the code that immediately follows will be compiled.

The general form of **#ifdef** is

#ifdef *macro-name*

If the *macro-name* has been defined in a **#define** statement, the code following the statement will be compiled.

The general form of **#ifndef** is

#ifndef *macro-name*

If *macro-name* is currently undefined by a **#define** statement, the code is compiled.

For example, here is the way some of these preprocessor directives work together. The following code will print "Hi Ted" and "Hi Jon" on the screen, but not "Hi George":

```
#define ted 10

// ...

#ifdef ted
  cout << "Hi Ted\n";
#endif
  cout << "Hi Jon\n";
#if 10<9
  cout << "Hi George\n";
#endif
```

The **#elif** directive is used to create an **if-else-if** statement. Its general form is

#elif *constant-expression*

You can string together a series of **#elifs** to handle several alternatives.

You can also use **#if** or **#elif** to determine if a macro name is defined by using the **defined** preprocessing operator. It takes this general form:

> #if defined *macro-name*
> *statement sequence*
> #endif

If the *macro-name* is defined, the statement sequence will be compiled. Otherwise it will be skipped. For example, the following fragment compiles the conditional code because **DEBUG** is defined by the program:

```
#define DEBUG
// ...
int i=100;
// ...
#if defined DEBUG
cout << "value of i is: " << i << endl;
#endif
```

You can also precede **defined** with the **!** operator to cause conditional compilation when the macro is not defined.

#include

The **#include** directive instructs the compiler to read and compile another source file. It takes these general forms:

> #include "*filename*"
>
> #include <*filename*>

The source file to be read in must be enclosed between double quotation marks or angle brackets. For example,

```
#include <stdio.h>
```

will instruct the compiler to read and compile the header for the C I/O functions.

If the filename is enclosed by angle brackets, the file is searched for in a manner defined by the creator of the compiler. Often, this means searching some special directory set aside for header files. If the filename is enclosed in quotes, the file is looked for in another implementation-defined manner. For many implementations, this means searching the current working directory. If the file is not found, the search is repeated as if the filename had been enclosed in angle brackets. You must check your compiler's user manual for details on the differences between angle brackets and double quotes. **#include** statements may be nested within other included files.

While all versions of C++ accept the form of **#include** statements just described, standard C++ has defined new-style headers that are used to include information about the standard C++ library. The new-style headers are not filenames. (Although they may map to filenames.) To include a new-style header, use this general form:

#include <*header-name*>

Here, *header-name* will be one of the new-style headers described in Chapter 2.

For example, to include the header information for the I/O system, use

#include <iostream>

Since the new-style headers are not filenames, they do not have .H extensions. Consult your compiler's documentation for more information about including the standard C++ headers in your C++ programs.

#line

The **#line** directive is used to change the contents of **__LINE__** and **__FILE__**, which are predefined identifiers. The basic form of the command is

#line *number* "*filename*"

where *number* is any positive integer and the *filename* is any valid file identifier. The value of *number* becomes the number of the current source line and *filename* becomes the name of the source file. The name of the file is optional. **#line** is primarily used for debugging purposes and special applications.

The **__LINE__** identifier is an integer, and **__FILE__** is a null-terminated string.

For example, the following code fragment sets the current line counter to 10 and the filename to "test":

```
#line 10 "test"
```

#pragma

The **#pragma** directive is an implementation-defined directive that allows various instructions to be given to the compiler. For example, a compiler may have an option to support the tracing of program execution. A trace option would then be specified by a **#pragma** statement. You must check your compiler's documentation for details and options.

#undef

The **#undef** directive removes a previously defined macro name. The general form is

#undef *macro-name*

For example, in the following code,

```
#define LEN 100
#define WIDTH 100

char array [LEN][WIDTH];

#undef LEN
#undef WIDTH
/* at this point both LEN and WIDTH are undefined */
```

both **LEN** and **WIDTH** are defined until the **#undef** statements are encountered.

THE # AND ## PREPROCESSOR OPERATORS

C/C++ provides two preprocessor operators: # and ##. These operators are used in a **#define** macro.

The # operator causes the argument it precedes to be turned into a quoted string. For example, consider the following program:

```
#include <iostream>
using namespace std;

#define mkstr(s)  # s

int main()
{
  cout << mkstr(I like C++);

  return 0;
}
```

The preprocessor turns the line

```
cout << mkstr(I like C++);
```

into

```
cout << "I like C++";
```

The ## operator is used to concatenate two tokens. For example, in the following program,

```
#include <iostream>
using namespace std;

#define concat(a, b)  a ## b

int main()
{
  int xy = 10;

  cout << concat(x, y);

  return 0;
}
```

the preprocessor transforms

```
cout << concat(x, y);
```

into

```
cout << xy;
```

If these operators seem strange to you, keep in mind that they are not needed or used in most programs. They exist primarily to allow some special cases to be handled by the preprocessor.

PREDEFINED MACRO NAMES

C/C++ specifies five built-in predefined macro names. They are

__LINE__

__FILE__

__DATE__

__TIME__

__cplusplus

The **__LINE__** and **__FILE__** macros are described in the **#line** discussion earlier in this chapter. The others will be examined here.

The **__DATE__** macro is a string, in the form *month/day/year,* that is the date of the translation of the source file into object code.

The time of the translation of the source code into object code is contained as a string in **__TIME__**. The form of the string is *hour:minute:second*.

The macro **__cplusplus** is defined when compiling a C++ program. This macro will not be defined by a C compiler. The macro **__STDC__** is defined when compiling a C program and can be defined by a C++ compiler. In both cases, check your compiler's documentation for details.

Most C/C++ compilers define several other built-in macros which relate to the specific environment and implementation.

COMMENTS

C++ defines two styles of comments. The first is a multiline comment. It begins with a /* and is terminated with a */. Anything between the comment symbols is ignored by the compiler. A multiline comment can extend over several lines.

The second type of comment is the single-line comment. It begins with a // and ends at the end of the line.

The multiline comment is the only type of comment supported by C. However, most C compilers will accept single-line comments even though it is nonstandard.

Chapter 5—Keyword Summary

The C language defines the following 32 keywords:

auto	double	int	struct
break	else	long	switch
case	enum	register	typedef
char	extern	return	union
const	float	short	unsigned
continue	for	signed	void
default	goto	sizeof	volatile
do	if	static	while

C++ includes all keywords defined by C and adds the following:

asm	inline	template
bool	mutable	this
catch	namespace	throw
class	new	true
const_cast	operator	try
delete	private	typeid
dynamic_cast	protected	typename
explicit	public	using
false	reinterpret_cast	virtual
friend	static_cast	wchar_t

Older versions of C++ also defined the keyword **overload**, but it is obsolete. All keywords are lowercase.

A brief synopsis of each of the keywords follows.

asm

asm is used to embed assembly language directly into your C++ program. The general form of the **asm** statement is shown here:

asm ("*instruction*");

Here, *instruction* is an assembly language instruction, which is passed directly to the compiler for assembly in your program.

Many C++ compilers allow additional forms of the **asm** statement. For example, Borland C++ allows the following **asm** statements:

```
asm instruction;
asm {
  instruction sequence
}
```

Here, *instruction sequence* is a list of assembly language instructions.

Note: Microsoft Visual C++ uses **__asm** *for embedding assembly code. It is otherwise similar to* **asm**.

auto

auto declares local variables. It is completely optional and seldom used.

bool

The type specifier **bool** is used to declare Boolean (i.e., true/false) values.

break

break is used to exit from a **do**, **for**, or **while** loop, bypassing the normal loop condition. It is also used to exit from a **switch** statement.

An example of **break** in a loop is shown here:

```
do {
  x = getx();
  if(x < 0) break; // terminate if negative
  process(x);
} while(!done);
```

Here, if **x** is negative, the loop is terminated.

In a **switch** statement, **break** keeps program execution from "falling through" to the next **case**. (Refer to "**switch**" later in this chapter for details.)

A **break** terminates only the **for**, **do**, **while**, or **switch** that contains it. It will not break out of any nested loops or **switch** statements.

case

The **case** statement is used with a **switch** statement. See "**switch**."

catch

The **catch** statement handles an exception generated by **throw**. See "**throw**."

char

char is a data type used to declare character variables.

class

class is used to declare classes—C++'s basic unit of encapsulation. Its general form is shown here:

```
class class-name : inheritance-list {
  // private members by default
protected:
  // private members that can be inherited
public:
  // public members
} object-list;
```

Here, *class-name* is the name of the new data type being generated by the **class** declaration. The *inheritance-list,* which is optional, specifies any base classes inherited by the new class. By default, members of a **class** are private. They can be made protected or public through the use of the **protected** and **public** keywords, respectively.

The *object-list* is optional. If not present, a class declaration simply specifies the form of a class. It does not create any objects of the class.

Note: For additional information on **class**, *see Chapter 1.*

const

The **const** modifier tells the compiler that a variable cannot be changed by your program. A **const** variable can, however, be given an initial value when it is declared.

const_cast

The **const_cast** operator is used to explicitly override **const** and/or **volatile** in a cast. It has this general form:

const_cast<*type*> (*object*)

The target type must be the same as the source type except for the alteration of its **const** or **volatile** attributes. The most common use of **const_cast** is to remove **const**-ness.

continue

continue is used to bypass portions of code in a loop and forces the conditional expression to be evaluated. For example, the following **while** loop will simply read characters from the keyboard until an **s** is typed.

```
while(ch = getchar()) {
  if(ch != 's') continue;  // read another char
  process(ch);
}
```

The call to **process( )** will not occur until **ch** contains the character **s**.

default

default is used in the **switch** statement to signal a default block of code to be executed if no matches are found in the **switch**. (See "**switch**.")

delete

The **delete** operator frees the memory pointed to by its argument. This memory must have previously been allocated using **new**. The general form of **delete** is

delete *p_var*;

where *p_var* is a pointer to previously allocated memory.

To free an array that has been allocated using **new**, use this general form of **delete**:

delete [ ] *p_var*;

do

The **do** loop is one of three loop constructs available in C++. The general form of the **do** loop is

```
do {
   statement block
} while(condition);
```

If only one statement is repeated, the braces are not necessary, but they do add clarity to the statement.

The **do** loop is the only loop in C++ that will always have at least one iteration because the condition is tested at the bottom of the loop.

double

double is a data type specifier used to declare double-precision floating-point variables.

dynamic_cast

dynamic_cast performs a runtime cast that verifies the validity of the cast. It has this general form:

dynamic_cast<*type*> (*object*)

The main use for **dynamic_cast** is to perform casts on polymorphic types. For example, given two polymorphic classes B and D, with D derived from B, a **dynamic_cast** can always cast a D* pointer into a B* pointer. A **dynamic_cast** can cast a B* pointer into a D* pointer only if the object being pointed to actually is a D*. In general, **dynamic_cast** will succeed if the attempted polymorphic cast is permitted (that is, if the target type can legally apply to the type of object being cast). If the cast cannot be made, then **dynamic_cast** evaluates to null.

else

See "**if**."

enum

The **enum** type specifier is used to create enumeration types. An enumeration is simply a list of named integer constants. The general form of an enumeration is shown here:

enum *name* {*name-list*} *var-list*;

The *name* is the type name of the enumeration. The *var-list* is optional, and enumeration variables can be declared separately from the type definition, as the following example shows. This code declares an enumeration called **color** and a variable of that type called **c**, and it performs an assignment and a conditional test.

```
enum color {red, green, yellow} c;

c = red;
if(c==red) cout << "is red\n";
```

Note: For more information on enumerations refer to Chapter 1.

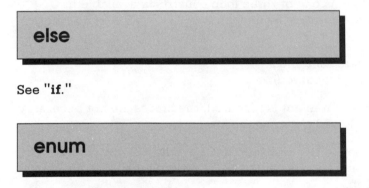

explicit

The **explicit** specifier applies only to constructors. A constructor specified as explicit will only be used when an initialization exactly matches that specified by the constructor. No automatic conversion will take place. (It creates a "nonconverting constructor.")

extern

extern is a data type modifier that tells the compiler about a variable that is defined elsewhere in the program. This is often used in conjunction with separately compiled files that share the same global data and are linked together. In essence, it notifies the compiler about the type of a variable without redefining it. For example, if **first** were defined in another file as an integer, the following declaration would be used in subsequent files:

```
extern int first;
```

This declaration specifies **first**'s type, but storage for it has not been created.

For C++ only, **extern** is also used to create a linkage specification. It has this general form:

extern "*language*" *function-prototype*

Here, *language* denotes the language to which you want the function to link. C and C++ linkages are guaranteed to be supported. Your compiler may support other linkages, too. To declare several functions using the same linkage specification, you can use this general form:

```
extern "language" {
  function-prototypes
}
```

false

false is the Boolean constant for false.

float

float is a data type specifier used to declare floating-point variables.

for

The **for** loop allows automatic initialization and incrementation of a counter variable. The general form is

```
for(initialization; condition; increment) {
  statement block
}
```

If the *statement block* is only one statement, the braces are not necessary.

Although **for** allows a number of variations, generally the *initialization* sets a loop control variable to its starting value. The *condition* is usually a relational statement that checks the loop control variable against a termination value, and *increment* increments (or decrements) it. If the *condition* is false to begin with, the body of the **for** loop will not execute even once.

The following statement will print the message "hello" ten times:

```
for(t=0; t<10; t++) cout << "hello\n";
```


friend

The keyword **friend** grants a nonmember function access to the private members of a class. To specify a friend function, include that function's prototype in the public section of a class declaration and precede the entire prototype with the keyword **friend**. For example, in the following class, **myfunc( )** is a friend, not a member, of **myclass**:

```
class myclass {
  // ...
public:
  friend void myfunc(int a, float b);
  // ...
};
```

Keep in mind that a **friend** function does not have a **this** pointer because it is not a member of the class.

goto

The **goto** keyword causes program execution to jump to the label specified in the **goto** statement. The general form of

goto is

goto *label*;
.
.
.
label:

All labels must end in a colon and must not conflict with keywords or function names. Furthermore, a **goto** can only branch within the current function—not from one function to another.

Programming Tip

Although the **goto** fell out of favor decades ago as a method of program control, it does occasionally have its uses. One of them is as a means of exiting from a deeply nested routine. For example, consider this fragment:

```
int i, j, k;
int stop = 0;

for(i=0; i<100 && !stop; i++) {
  for(j=0; j<10 && !stop; j++) {
    for(k=0; k<20; k++) {
      // ...
      if(something()) {
        stop = 1;
        break;
      }
    }
  }
}
```

As you can see, the variable **stop** is used to cancel the two outer loops if some program event occurs. However, a better way to accomplish this is shown here, using **goto**:

```
int i, j, k;

for(i=0; i<100; i++) {
  for(j=0; j<10; j++) {
    for(k=0; k<20; k++) {
      // ...
      if(something()) {
        goto done;
      }
    }
  }
}

done: // ...
```

As you can see, the use of **goto** eliminates the extra overhead that was added by the repeated testing of **stop** in the previous version.

While using **goto** as a general-purpose form of loop control should be avoided, it can sometimes be employed with great success.

if

The **if** keyword allows a course of action to be based on the outcome of a condition. The general form of the **if** statement is

if(*condition*) {
  statement block 1
}
else {
  statement block 2
}

If single statements are used, the braces are not needed. The **else** is optional.

The *condition* can be any expression. If that expression evaluates to true (any value other than zero), then *statement block 1* will be executed; otherwise, if it exists, *statement block 2* will be executed.

The following fragment checks to see if **x** is greater than 10:

```
if(x > 10)
  cout << "x is greater than 10.";
else
  cout << "x is less than or equal to 10.";
```

inline

The **inline** specifier tells the compiler to expand a function's code inline rather than calling the function. The **inline** specifier is a request, not a command, because several factors can prevent a function's code from being expanded inline. Some common restrictions include recursive functions, functions that contain loops or **switch** statements, and functions that contain static data. The **inline** specifier precedes the rest of a function's declaration.

The following fragment tells the compiler to generate inline code for **myfunc( )**:

```
inline void myfunc(int i)
{
  // ...
}
```

When a function's definition is included within a class declaration, that function's code is automatically in-lined, if possible.

int

int is the type specifier used to declare integer variables.

long

long is a data type modifier used to declare long integer variables.

mutable

The **mutable** specifier allows a member of an object to override **const**ness. That is, a **mutable** member of a **const** object is not **const** and can be modified. The main use of **mutable** is to allow a **const** member function to modify selected data members.

namespace

The **namespace** keyword allows you to partition the global namespace by creating a declarative region. In essence, a namespace defines a scope. The general form of **namespace** is shown here:

```
namespace name {
  // declarations
}
```

In addition, you can have unnamed namespaces, as shown here:

```
namespace {
  // declarations
}
```

Unnamed namespaces allow you to establish unique identifiers that are known only within the scope of a single file.

Here is an example of a **namespace**:

```
namespace MyNameSpace {
  int i, k;
  void myfunc(int j) { cout << j; }
}
```

Here, **i**, **k**, and **myfunc( )** are part of the scope defined by the **MyNameSpace** namespace.

Since a namespace defines a scope, you need to use the scope resolution operator to refer to objects defined within one. For example, to assign the value 10 to **i**, you must use this statement:

```
MyNameSpace::i = 10;
```

If the members of a namespace will be frequently used, you can use a **using** directive to simplify their access. The **using** statement has these two general forms:

using namespace *name*;

using *name*:: *member*;

In the first form, *name* specifies the name of the namespace you want to access. All of the members defined within the specified namespace can be used without qualification. In the second form, only a specific member of the namespace is made visible. For example, assuming **MyNameSpace** as shown above, the following **using** statements and assignments are valid:

```
using MyNameSpace::k; // only k is made visible
k = 10; // OK because k is visible

using namespace MyNameSpace;
  // all members of MyNameSpace are visible
i = 10;
  // OK because all members of MyNameSpace are now visible
```


new

The **new** operator allocates dynamic memory and returns a pointer of the appropriate type to it. Its general form is shown here:

p_var = new *type*;

Here, *p_var* is a pointer variable that will receive the address of the allocated memory, and *type* is the type of data that the memory will hold. The **new** operator automatically allocates sufficient memory to hold one item of data of the specified type. For example, the following code fragment allocates sufficient memory to hold a **double**:

```
double *p;

p = new double;
```

If the allocation request fails, one of two events will occur. Either a null pointer is returned or a **bad_alloc** exception is thrown. (Currently, some compilers throw an **xalloc** exception.)

Note: At the time of this writing, the precise behavior of **new** *on failure is still being refined. Furthermore, different compilers exhibit different behaviors on allocation failure. Check your compiler's documentation for information that applies to your current working environment.*

You can initialize the allocated memory by specifying an initializer, using this general form:

p_var = new *type* (*initializer*);

Here, *initializer* is the value that will be assigned to the allocated memory.

To allocate a single-dimension array, use the following general form:

p_var = new *type*[*size*];

Here, *size* specifies the length of the array. **new** will automatically allocate sufficient room to hold an array of the specified type and of the specified size. When allocating arrays, no initializations can be given.

operator

The **operator** keyword is used to create overloaded operator functions. Operator functions come in two varieties: member and nonmember. The general form of a member operator function is shown here:

```
ret-type class-name::operator#( param-list) {
  // ...
}
```

Here, *ret-type* is the return type of the function, *class-name* is the name of the class for which the operator is overloaded, and # is the operator to be overloaded. When overloading a unary operator, the *param-list* is empty. (The operand is passed implicitly in **this**.) When overloading a binary operator, the *param-list* specifies the operand on the right side of the operator. (The operand on the left is passed implicitly in **this**.)

For nonmember functions, an operator function has this general form:

```
ret-type operator#( param-list) {
  // ...
}
```

Here, *param-list* contains one parameter when overloading a unary operator and two parameters when overloading a binary operator. When overloading a binary operator, the operand on the left is passed in the first parameter, and the operand on the right is passed in the right parameter.

Several restrictions apply to operator overloading. First, you cannot alter the precedence of the operator. You cannot change the number of operands required by an operator. You cannot change the meaning of an operator relative to C++'s built-in data types. You cannot create a new operator. The preprocessor operators # and ## cannot be overloaded. You cannot overload the following operators:

```
. : .* ?
```

private

The **private** access specifier declares private members of a class. It is also used to inherit a base class privately. When used to declare private members, it has this general form:

```
class class-name {
  // ...
private:
  // private members
};
```

Members of a **class** are private by default. Thus, the access specifier **private** will only be used in a **class** declaration to begin another block of private declarations. For example, this is a valid class declaration:

```
class myclass {
  int a, b; // private by default
public: // begin public declarations
  int x, y; // these are public
private: // return to private declarations
  int c, d; // these are private
};
```

When used as an inheritance specifier, **private** has this general form:

class *class-name* : private *base-class* { // ...

By specifying a base class as **private**, all public and protected members of the base class become private members of the derived class. All private members of the base class remain private to it.

protected

The **protected** access specifier declares members in a class that are private to that class but can be inherited by any derived class. It has the following general form:

```
class class-name {
  // ...
protected: // make protected
  // protected members
};
```

For example,

```
class base {
  // ...
protected:
  int a;
  // ...
};

// Now, inherit base into derived class.
class derived : public base {
  // ...
public:
  // ...
  // derived has access to a
  voidf() { cout << a; }
};
```

Here, **a** is private to **base** and cannot be accessed by any nonmember function. However, **derived** inherits access to **a**. If **a** were simply defined as **private**, **derived** would not have access to it.

When used as an inheritance specifier, **protected** has this general form:

> class *class- name* : protected *base-class* { // ...

By specifying a base class as **protected**, all public and protected members of the base class become protected members of the derived class. In all cases, private members of the base class remain private to that base.

public

The **public** access specifier declares public members of a class. It is also used to publicly inherit a base class. When used to declare public members, it has this general form:

```
class class-name {
  // private members by default
public: // make public
  // public members
};
```

Members of a **class** are private by default. To declare public members of a **class**, you must specify them as **public**.

When used as an inheritance specifier, **public** has this general form:

```
class class-name : public base-class { // ...
```

By specifying a base class as **public**, all public members of the base class become public members of the derived class, and all protected members of the base class become protected members of the derived class. In all cases, private members of the base class remain private to that base.

register

The **register** storage class modifier requests that access to a variable be optimized for speed. Traditionally, **register** applied only to integer or character variables, causing them to be stored in a register of the CPU instead of being placed in memory. The meaning of **register** has since been broadened to include all types of data. However, data other than integers and characters cannot usually be stored in a CPU register. For other types of data, either cache memory (or some other sort of optimizing scheme) is used, or the **register** request is ignored.

register can only be used on local variables. In C, you cannot take the address of a **register** variable. However, in C++, you can (although doing so may prevent the variable from being optimized).

reinterpret_cast

The **reinterpret_cast** operator changes one type into a fundamentally different type. For example, it can be used to change a pointer into an integer. It has this general form:

reinterpret_cast<*type*> (*object*)

A **reinterpret_cast** should be used for casting inherently incompatible pointer types.

return

The **return** statement forces a return from a function and can be used to transfer a value back to the calling routine. It has these two forms:

return;
return *value*;

In C++, the form of **return** that does not specify a value must only be used in **void** functions.

The following function returns the product of its two integer arguments:

```
int mul(int a, int b)
{
  return a*b;
}
```

Keep in mind that as soon as a **return** is encountered, the function will return, skipping any other code that may be in the function.

Also, a function can contain more than one **return** statement.

short

short is a data type modifier used to declare short integers.

signed

The principal use of the **signed** type modifier is to specify a **signed char** data type. Its use on other integer types is redundant since integers are signed, by default.

sizeof

The **sizeof** compile-time operator returns the length (in bytes) of the variable or type it precedes. If it precedes a type, that type must be enclosed in parentheses. If it precedes a variable, the parentheses are optional. For example, given

```
int i;
cout << sizeof(int);
cout << sizeof i;
```

both output statements will print 4 for most 32-bit C++ compilers.

static

static is a data type modifier that creates permanent storage for the local variable that it precedes. This enables the specified variable to maintain its value between function calls.

static can also be used to declare global variables. In this case, it limits the scope of the variable that it modifies to the file in which it is declared.

In C++, when **static** is used on a class data member, it causes only one copy of that member to be shared by all objects of its class.

static_cast

The **static_cast** operator performs a nonpolymorphic cast. For example, it can be used to cast a base class pointer into a derived class pointer. It can also be used for any standard conversion. No runtime checks are performed. It has this general form:

static_cast<*type*> (*object*)

struct

The **struct** keyword is used to create an aggregate data type called a *structure.* In C++, a structure can contain both function and data members. In C++, a structure has the same capabilities as a **class** except that, by default, its members are public rather than private. The general form of a C++ structure is

struct *class-name* : *inheritance-list*{
  // public members by default
protected:
  // private members that can be inherited
private:
  // private members
} *object-list*;

The *class-name* is the type name of the structure, which is a class type. The individual members are referenced using the dot when operating on a structure or by using the arrow operator when operating through a pointer to the structure. The *object-list* and *inheritance-list* are optional.

In C, structures can only contain data members, the **private** and **protected** specifiers are not allowed, and no inheritance list is allowed.

The following C-style structure contains a string called **name** and two integers called **high** and **low**. It also declares one variable called **my_var**.

```
struct my_struct {
  char name[80];
  int high;
  int low;
} my_var;
```

Note: See Chapter 1 for more detailed coverage of structures.

switch

The **switch** statement is C/C++'s multiway branch statement. It is used to route execution one of several different ways. The general form of the statement is

> switch (*expression*) {
>   case *constant 1*: *statement sequence 1*;
>   *break*;
>   case *constant 2*: *statement sequence 2*;
>   break;
>   .
>   .
>   .
>   case *constant N*: *statement sequence N*;
>   break;
>   default: *default statements*;
> }

Each statement sequence can be from one to several statements long. The **default** portion is optional. Both *expression* and the **case** constants must be integral types.

The **switch** works by checking the *expression* against the constants. If a match is found, that sequence of statements is executed. If the statement sequence associated with the matching **case** does not contain a **break**, execution will continue on into the next **case**. Put differently, from the point of the match, execution will continue until either a **break** statement is found or the **switch** ends. If no match is found and a **default** case exists, its statement sequence is executed. Otherwise, no action takes place. The following example processes a menu selection:

```
switch(ch) {
  case 'e': enter();
    break;
  case 'l': list();
    break;
  case 's': sort();
    break;
  case 'q': exit(0);
    break;
```

```
  default:
    cout << "Unknown command!\n";
    cout << "Try Again.\n";
}
```

template

The **template** keyword is used to create generic functions and classes. The type of data operated upon by a generic function or class is specified as a parameter. Thus, one function or class definition can be used with several different types of data. The details concerning template functions and classes follow.

A generic function defines a general set of operations that can be applied to various types of data. A generic function has the type of data that it will operate upon passed to it as a parameter. Using this mechanism, the same general procedure can be applied to a wide range of data. As you know, many algorithms are logically the same no matter what type of data is being operated upon. For example, the Quicksort algorithm is the same whether it is applied to an array of integers or an array of floating-point numbers. It is just the type of the data being sorted that is different. By creating a generic function, you can define, independent of any data, the nature of the algorithm. Once this is done, the compiler automatically generates the correct code for the type of data that is actually used when you execute the function. In essence, when you create a generic function you are creating a function that can automatically overload itself.

The general form of a **template** function definition is shown here:

template <class *data-type*> *ret-type func-name(parameter list)*
{
  // body of function
}

Here, *data-type* is a placeholder for the type of data upon which the function will actually operate.

Here is an example. The following program creates a generic function that swaps the values of the two variables it is called with. Because the general process of exchanging two values is independent of the type of the variables, it is a good candidate to be made into a generic function.


```
// Function template example.
#include <iostream>
using namespace std;

// Here is a template function.
template <class X> void swapvals(X &a, X &b)
{
  X temp;

  temp = a;
  a = b;
  b = temp;
}

int main()
{
  int i=10, j=20;
  float x=10.1, y=23.3;

  cout << "Original i, j: " << i << ' ' << j
       <<  endl;
  cout << "Original x, y: " << x << ' ' << y
       << endl;

  swapvals(i, j); // swap integers
  swapvals(x, y); // swap floats

  cout << "Swapped i, j: " << i << ' ' << j
       << endl;
  cout << "Swapped x, y: " << x << ' ' << y
       << endl;

  return 0;
}
```

In this program, the line

```
template <class X> void swapvals(X &a, X &b)
```

tells the compiler two things: first, that a template function is being created, and second, that **X** is a generic type that is used as a placeholder. The body of **swapvals( )** is defined using **X** as the data type of the values that will be swapped. In **main( )**, the **swapvals( )** function is called using two different types of data: integers and floating-point numbers. Because **swapvals( )** is a generic function, the compiler automatically creates two versions of **swapvals( )**—one that will exchange integer values and one that will exchange floating-point values.

You can define more than one generic type using the **template** statement, with a comma-separated list.

Generic functions are similar to overloaded functions except that they are more restrictive. When functions are overloaded, you can have different actions performed within the body of each function. A generic function must perform the same general action for all versions.

In addition to generic functions, you can also define a *generic class*. When you do this, you create a class that defines all algorithms used by that class, but the actual type of the data being manipulated will be specified as a parameter when objects of that class are created.

Generic classes are useful when a class contains generalizable logic. For example, the same algorithm that maintains a queue of integers will also work for a queue of characters. Also, the same mechanism that maintains a linked list of mailing addresses will also maintain a linked list of auto parts. By using a generic class, you can create a class that will maintain a queue, linked list, and so on for any type of data. The compiler will automatically generate the correct type of object based upon the type you specify when the object is created.

Here is the general form of a generic class declaration:

> template <class *data_type*> class *class-name* {
>   // ...
> };

In this case, *data_type* is a placeholder for a type of data that the class will operate on. When you declare an object of a generic class, you specify the type of data between angle brackets, using this general form:

> *class-name*<*type*> *object*;

The following is an example of a generic class. This program creates a very simple generic singly linked list class. It then demonstrates the class by creating a linked list that stores characters.

```
// A simple generic linked list.
#include <iostream>
using namespace std;

template <class data_t> class list {
  data_t data;
  list *next;
public:
  list(data_t d);
  void add(list *node) { node->next = this;
                         next = 0; }
  list *getnext() { return next; }
  data_t getdata() { return data; }
};

template <class data_t>
list<data_t>::list(data_t d)
{
  data = d;
  next = 0;
}
```

```
int main()
{
  list<char> start('a');
  list<char> *p, *last;
  int i;

  // build a list
  last = &start;
  for(i=0; i<26; i++) {
    p = new list<char> ('a' + i);
    p->add(last);
    last = p;
  }

  // follow the list
  p = &start;
  while(p) {
    cout << p->getdata();
    p = p->getnext();
  }

  return 0;
}
```

As you can see, the declaration of a generic class is similar to that of a generic function. The type of data stored by the list is made generic in the class declaration. In **main( )**, objects and pointers are created that specify that the data type of the list will be **char**. Lists of other types can also be created.

Pay special attention to this declaration:

```
list<char> start('a');
```

Notice how the desired data type is passed inside the angle brackets.

this

this is a pointer to the object that generated a call to a member function. All member functions are automatically passed a **this** pointer.

throw

throw is part of C++'s exception handling subsystem. A general description follows.

Exception handling is built upon three keywords: **try**, **catch**, and **throw**. In the most general terms, program statements that you want to monitor for exceptions are contained in a **try** block. If an exception (that is, an error) occurs within the **try** block, it is thrown (using **throw**). The exception is caught, using **catch**, and processed. The following discussion elaborates on this general description.

As stated, any statement that throws an exception must have been executed from within a **try** block. (Functions called from within a **try** block may also throw an exception.) Any exception must be caught by a **catch** statement that immediately follows the **try** statement that throws the exception. The general form of **try** and **catch** is shown here:

```
try {
  // try block
}
catch (type1 arg) {
  // catch block
}
```

```
catch (type2 arg) {
  // catch block
}
catch (type3 arg) {
  // catch block
}
// ...
catch (typeN arg) {
  // catch block
}
```

The **try** block must contain that portion of your program that you want to monitor for errors. This can be as short as a few statements within one function or as all-encompassing as enclosing the **main( )** function code within a **try** block (which effectively causes the entire program to be monitored).

When an exception is thrown, it is caught by its corresponding **catch** statement, which processes the exception. There can be more than one **catch** statement associated with a **try**. Which **catch** statement is used is determined by the type of the exception. That is, if the data type specified by a **catch** matches that of the exception, then that **catch** statement is executed (and all others are bypassed). When an exception is caught, *arg* will receive its value. Any type of data can be caught, including classes that you create. If no exception is thrown (that is, no error occurs within the **try** block), then no **catch** statement is executed.

The general form of the **throw** statement is shown here:

```
throw exception;
```

throw must be executed either from within the **try** block itself or from any function called (directly or indirectly) from within the **try** block. *exception* is the value thrown.

If you throw an exception for which there is no applicable **catch** statement, an abnormal program termination may occur.

Throwing an unhandled exception causes the **terminate( )** function to be invoked. By default, **terminate( )** calls **abort( )** to stop your program. However, you can specify your own handlers if you like, using **set_terminate( )**.

Here is a simple example that shows the way C++ exception handling operates:

```
// A simple exception handling example.
#include <iostream>
using namespace std;

int main()
{
  cout << "Start\n";

  try { // start a try block
    cout << "Inside try block\n";
    throw 100; // throw an error
    cout << "This will not execute";
  }
  catch (int i) { // catch an error
    cout << "Caught an exception -- value is: ";
    cout << i << "\n";
  }

  cout << "End";

  return 0;
}
```

This program displays the following output:

```
Start
Inside try block
Caught an exception -- value is: 100
End
```

As you can see, there is a **try** block containing three statements and a **catch(int i)** statement that processes an integer exception. Within the **try** block, only two of the three statements will execute: the first **cout** statement and the **throw**. Once an exception has been thrown, control passes to the **catch** expression and the **try** block is terminated. That is, **catch** is *not* called. Rather, program execution is transferred to it. (The program's stack is automatically reset as needed to accomplish this.) Thus, the **cout** statement following the **throw** will never execute.

true

true is the Boolean constant for true.

try

try is part of C++'s exception-handling mechanism. See "**throw**."

typedef

The **typedef** keyword allows you to create a new name for an existing data type. The data type can be either one of the built-in types, or a class, structure, union, or enumeration. The general form of **typedef** is

typedef *type_specifier new_name*;

For example, to use the word **balance** in place of **float**, you would write

```
typedef float balance;
```

typeid

In C++, the **typeid** operator returns a reference to a **type_info** object that describes the type of the object to which **typeid** is being applied. **typeid** has this general form:

typeid(*object*)

typeid supports run-time type identification (RTTI) in C++.

Note: See "**typeid**" *in Chapter 3.*

typename

C++ supports the **typename** keyword. It can be used in place of the keyword **class** in a **template** declaration or to signify an undefined type.

union

A union is a special type of class that assigns two or more variables to the same memory location. The form of the definition and the way the **.** (dot) and –> (arrow) operators reference a member are the same as for a **class**. By default, its members are public. The general form is

```
union class-name {
  // public members by default
private:
  // private members
} object-list;
```

The *class-name* is the type name for the union.

Note: In C, unions can only contain data members, and the **private** *specifier is not allowed. Thus, C unions can only contain data.*

For example, the following code creates a union between a **double** and a character string and creates one variable called **my_var**:

```
union my_union {
  char time[30];
  double offset;
} my_var;
```

Unions are covered in more detail in Chapter 1.

unsigned

unsigned is a data type modifier that declares unsigned integers. Unsigned integers can hold only positive values.

using

See **namespace**.

virtual

The **virtual** function specifier creates a virtual function. A virtual function is a member of a base class that can be overridden by a derived class. If the function is not overridden by a derived class, the base class' definition is used.

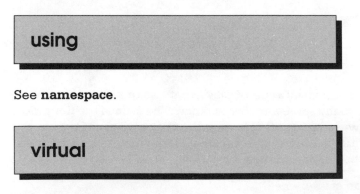

A *pure virtual function* is a member function that has no definition. This means that a pure virtual function *must be* overridden in a derived class. A pure virtual function is prototyped like this:

virtual *ret-type fname*(*param-list*) = 0;

Here, *ret-type* is the return type of the function, *fname* is the function's name, and *param-list* specifies any parameters. The important feature is the **= 0**. This tells the compiler that the virtual function has no definition relative to the base class.

Runtime polymorphism is attained when virtual functions are accessed through a base class pointer. When this is done, the type of object pointed to determines which version of the virtual function is called.

Programming Tip

A class that contains at least one pure virtual function is called *abstract.* Abstract classes cannot be used to instantiate objects. They also cannot be used as function parameter types or as return types. However, you can create a pointer to an abstract class.

A class that inherits an abstract class and does not override all of the pure virtual functions will, itself, be abstract. A derived class must override all pure virtual functions of all of its base classes before the derived class becomes concrete and objects of its class can be created.

void

The **void** type specifier is primarily used to explicitly declare functions that return no value. It is also used to create **void** pointers (pointers to **void**), which are generic pointers that are capable of pointing to any type of object.

In C, **void** is also used to declare an empty parameter list in a function declaration.

volatile

The **volatile** modifier tells the compiler that a variable can have its contents altered in ways not explicitly defined by the program. For example, variables that are changed by hardware such as real-time clocks, interrupts, or other inputs should be declared as **volatile**.

wchar_t

wchar_t specifies a wide-character type. Wide characters are 16 bits long.

while

The **while** loop has the general form,

```
while(condition) {
  statement block
}
```

If a single statement is the object of the **while**, then the braces can be omitted.

The **while** tests the *condition* at the top of the loop. Therefore, if the *condition* is false to begin with, the loop will not execute even once. The *condition* can be any expression.

The following is an example of a **while** loop. It will read 100 characters and store them into a character array.


```
char s[256];

t = 0;
while(t<100) {
  s[t] = stream.get();
  t++;
}
```

Chapter 6—The Standard C I/O Functions

This chapter describes the standard C I/O functions. These functions are defined by the ANSI C standard, and all C compilers supply them in their standard libraries. They are also supported by C++ to provide compatibility with C, and there is no fundamental reason that you cannot use them in your C++ program when you deem it appropriate. Because the functions in this chapter are specified by the ANSI C standard, they will be referred to collectively as the *ANSI C I/O system.*

The header file associated with the standard I/O functions is called STDIO.H. It defines several macros and types used by the file system. The most important type is **FILE**, which is used to declare a file pointer. Two other types are **size_t** and **fpos_t**, which are some form of unsigned integer. The **size_t** type defines an object that is capable of holding the size of the largest file allowed by the operating environment. The **fpos_t** type defines an object that can hold all information needed to uniquely specify every position within a file.

The ANSI C I/O system operates through *streams.* A stream is a logical device that is connected to an actual physical device, which is referred to as the *file*.

In the ANSI C I/O system, all streams have the same capabilities, but files can have differing qualities. For example, a disk file allows random access, but a modem does not. Thus, the ANSI C I/O system provides a level of abstraction between the programmer and the physical device. The abstraction is the stream, and the device is the file. In this way, a consistent logical interface can be maintained, even though the actual physical devices may differ.

A stream is connected to a file via a call to **fopen( )**. Streams are operated upon through a file pointer (which is a pointer of type **FILE ***). In a sense, the file pointer is the glue that holds the system together.

When your program begins execution, three predefined streams are automatically opened. They are **stdin**, **stdout**, and **stderr**, referring to standard input, standard output, and standard error, respectively. By default, these are connected to the console, but they can be redirected to any other type of device.

Many of the standard library I/O functions set the built-in global integer variable **errno** when an error occurs. Your program can check this variable when an error occurs to obtain more information about the error. The values that **errno** can take are implementation-dependent.

clearerr

```
#include <stdio.h>
void clearerr(FILE *stream);
```

The **clearerr( )** function resets (i.e., sets to zero) the error flag associated with the stream pointed to by *stream.* The end-of-file indicator is also reset.

The error flags for each stream are initially set to zero by a successful call to **fopen( )**. Once an error has occurred, the flags stay set until an explicit call to either **clearerr( )** or **rewind( )** is made.

File errors can occur for a wide variety of reasons, many of which are system-dependent. The exact nature of the error can be determined by calling **perror( )**, which displays what error has occurred (see "**perror( )**").

Related functions are **feof( )**, **ferror( )**, and **perror( )**.

fclose

```
#include <stdio.h>
int fclose(FILE *stream);
```

The **fclose( )** function closes the file associated with *stream* and flushes its buffer. After an **fclose( )**, *stream* is no longer connected with the file, and any automatically allocated buffers are deallocated.

If **fclose( )** is successful, zero is returned; otherwise **EOF** is returned. Trying to close a file that has already been closed is an error. Removing the storage media before closing a file will also generate an error, as will lack of sufficient free disk space.

Related functions are **fopen( )**, **freopen( )**, and **fflush( )**.

feof

```
#include <stdio.h>
int feof(FILE *stream);
```

The **feof( )** function checks the file position indicator to determine if the end of the file associated with *stream* has been reached. A nonzero value is returned if the file position indicator is at end-of-file; zero is returned otherwise.

Once the end of the file has been reached, subsequent read operations will return **EOF** until either **rewind( )** is called or the file position indicator is moved using **fseek( )**. The macro **EOF** is defined in STDIO.H.

The **feof( )** function is particularly useful when working with binary files because the end-of-file marker is also a valid binary integer. Explicit calls must be made to **feof( )** rather than simply testing the return value of **getc( )**, for example, to determine when the end of a binary file has been reached.

Related functions are **clearerr( )**, **ferror( )**, **perror( )**, **putc( )**, and **getc( )**.

ferror

```
#include <stdio.h>
int ferror(FILE *stream);
```

The **ferror( )** function checks for a file error on the given *stream*. A return value of zero indicates that no error has occurred, while a nonzero value means an error.

The error flags associated with *stream* will stay set until either the file is closed or **rewind( )** or **clearerr( )** is called.

To determine the exact nature of the error, use the **perror( )** function.

Related functions are **clearerr( )**, **feof( )**, and **perror( )**.

fflush

```
#include <stdio.h>
int fflush(FILE *stream);
```

If *stream* is associated with a file opened for writing, a call to **fflush( )** causes the contents of the output buffer to be physically written to the file. If *stream* points to an input file, the contents of the input buffer are cleared. In either case, the file remains open.

A return value of zero indicates success; **EOF** indicates that a write error has occurred.

All buffers are automatically flushed upon normal termination of the program or when they are full. Also, closing a file flushes its buffer.

Related functions are **fclose( )**, **fopen( )**, **fread( )**, **fwrite( )**, **getc( )**, and **putc( )**.

fgetc

```
#include <stdio.h>
int fgetc(FILE *stream);
```

The **fgetc( )** function returns the next character from the input *stream* at the current position and increments the file position indicator. The character is read as an **unsigned char** that is converted to an integer.

If the end of the file is reached, **fgetc( )** returns **EOF**. However, since **EOF** is a valid integer value, when working with binary files you must use **feof( )** to check for the end of the file. If **fgetc( )** encounters an error, **EOF** is also returned. If working with binary files, you must use **ferror( )** to check for file errors.

Related functions are **fputc( )**, **getc( )**, **putc( )**, and **fopen( )**.

fgetpos

```
#include <stdio.h>
int fgetpos(FILE *stream, fpos_t *position);
```

The **fgetpos( )** function stores the current value of the file position indicator in the object pointed to by *position*. The object pointed to by *position* must be of type **fpos_t**, which is a type defined in STDIO.H. The value stored there is useful only in a subsequent call to **fsetpos( )**.

If an error occurs, **fgetpos( )** returns nonzero; otherwise it returns zero.

Related functions are **fsetpos( )**, **fseek( )**, and **ftell( )**.

fgets

```
#include <stdio.h>
char *fgets(char *str, int num, FILE *stream);
```

The **fgets( )** function reads up to *num* – 1 characters from *stream* and places them into the character array pointed to by *str*. Characters are read until either a newline or an **EOF** is received or until the specified limit is reached. After the characters have been read, a null is placed in the array immediately after the last character read. A newline character will be retained and will be part of *str*.

If successful, **fgets( )** returns *str;* a null pointer is returned upon failure. If a read error occurs, the contents of the array pointed to by *str* are indeterminate. Because a null pointer will be returned either when an error occurs or when the end of the file is reached, you should use **feof( )** or **ferror( )** to determine what has actually happened.

Related functions are **fputs( )**, **fgetc( )**, **gets( )**, and **puts( )**.

fopen

```
#include <stdio.h>
FILE *fopen(const char *fname, const char *mode);
```

The **fopen( )** function opens a file whose name is pointed to by *fname* and returns the stream that is associated with it. The types of operations that will be allowed on the file are defined by the value of *mode*. The legal values for *mode* are shown in the following table. The filename must be a string of characters constituting a valid filename as defined by the operating system and can include a path specification if the environment supports it.

Mode	Meaning
"r"	Open text file for reading
"w"	Create text file for writing
"a"	Append to text file
"rb"	Open binary file for reading
"wb"	Create binary file for writing
"ab"	Append to binary file
"r+"	Open text file for read/write
"w+"	Create text file for read/write
"a+"	Open text file for read/write
"rb+"	Open binary file for read/write
"wb+"	Create binary file for read/write
"ab+"	Open binary file for read/write

If **fopen( )** is successful in opening the specified file, a **FILE** pointer is returned. If the file cannot be opened, a null pointer is returned.

As the table shows, a file can be opened in either text or binary mode. In text mode, some character translations can occur. For example, newlines can be converted into carriage return/linefeed sequences. No such translations occur on binary files.

The correct method of opening a file is illustrated by this code fragment:

```
FILE *fp;

if ((fp = fopen("test", "w"))==NULL) {
  printf("Cannot open file.\n");
  exit(1);
}
```

This method detects any error in opening a file, such as a write-protected or full disk, before attempting to write to it. **NULL** is used to indicate an error because no file pointer will ever have that value. **NULL** is defined in STDIO.H.

If you use **fopen( )** to open a file for output, any preexisting file by that name will be erased and a new file started. If no file by that name exists, one will be created. If you want to add to the end of the file, you must use mode "a". If the file does not exist, an error will be returned. Opening a file for read operations requires that the file exist. If it does not exist, an error will be returned. Finally, if a file is opened for read/write operations, it will not be erased if it exists; however, if it does not exist it will be created.

When accessing a file opened for read/write operations, you cannot follow an output operation with an input operation without an intervening call to either **fflush( )**, **fseek( )**, **fsetpos( )**, or **rewind( )**. Also, you cannot follow an input operation with an output operation without an intervening call to one of the previously mentioned functions.

Related functions are **fclose( )**, **fread( )**, **fwrite( )**, **putc( )**, and **getc( )**.

Programming Tip

Any file can be opened as either a text file or a binary file. It does not matter what the file actually contains. For example, a file that holds ASCII text can still be opened and operated upon as a binary file. As far as the ANSI C file system is concerned, the only difference between a text file and a binary file is that no character translations will take place when operating on a file opened in binary mode.

You might want to open a file that contains text as a binary file when you are performing various non-text-based manipulations on it. For example, file utilities that compare, compress, or sort will typically open the files for binary access. Also, file encryption programs will almost always need to operate in binary mode.

The key point is that the difference between a text file and a binary file is not what the file contains but rather the mode in which you open it.

fprintf

```
#include <stdio.h>
int fprintf(FILE *stream, const char *format, ...);
```

The **fprintf( )** function outputs the values of the arguments that compose the argument list as specified in the *format* string to the stream pointed to by *stream.* The return value is the number of characters actually printed. If an error occurs, a negative number is returned.

There can be from zero to several arguments, with the maximum number being system dependent.

The operations of the format control string and commands are identical to those in **printf( )**; see "**printf( )**" for a complete description.

Related functions are **printf( )** and **fscanf( )**.

fputc

```
#include <stdio.h>
int fputc(int ch, FILE *stream);
```

The **fputc( )** function writes the character *ch* to the specified stream at the current file position and then advances the file position indicator. Even though *ch* is declared to be an **int** for historical reasons, it is converted by **fputc( )** into an **unsigned char**. Because all character arguments are elevated to integers at the time of the call, you are free to use character variables as arguments. If an integer were used, the high-order byte would simply be discarded.

The value returned by **fputc( )** is the value of the character written. If an error occurs, **EOF** is returned. For files opened for binary operations, an **EOF** may be a valid character, and the function **ferror( )** will need to be used to determine whether an error has actually occurred.

Related functions are **fgetc( )**, **fopen( )**, **fprintf( )**, **fread( )**, and **fwrite( )**.

fputs

```
#include <stdio.h>
int fputs(const char *str, FILE *stream);
```

The **fputs( )** function writes the contents of the string pointed to by *str* to the specified stream. The null terminator is not written.

The **fputs( )** function returns nonnegative on success and **EOF** on failure.

If the stream is opened in text mode, certain character translations may take place. This means that there may not be a one-to-one mapping of the string onto the file. However, if the stream is opened in binary mode, no character translations will occur, and a one-to-one mapping between the string and the file will exist.

Related functions are **fgets( )**, **gets( )**, **puts( )**, **fprintf( )**, and **fscanf( )**.

fread

```
#include <stdio.h>
int fread(void *buf, size_t size, size_t count,
          FILE *stream);
```

The **fread( )** function reads *count* number of objects, each object being *size* bytes in length, from the stream pointed to by *stream* and places them in the array pointed to by *buf.* The file position indicator is advanced by the number of characters read.

The **fread( )** function returns the number of items actually read. If fewer items are read than are requested in the call, either an error has occurred or the end of the file has been reached. You must use **feof( )** or **ferror( )** to determine what has taken place.

If the stream is opened for text operations, certain character translations, such as carriage return/linefeed sequences being transformed into newlines, may occur.

Related functions are **fwrite( )**, **fopen( )**, **fscanf( )**, **fgetc( )**, and **getc( )**.

freopen

```
#include <stdio.h>
FILE *freopen(const char *fname, const char *mode,
              FILE *stream);
```

The **freopen( )** function associates an existing stream with a different file. The new file's name is pointed to by *fname,* the access mode is pointed to by *mode,* and the stream to be reassigned is pointed to by *stream*. The string *mode* uses the same format as **fopen( )**; a complete discussion is found in the "**fopen( )**" section.

When called, **freopen( )** first tries to close a file that may currently be associated with *stream.* However, if the attempt to close the file fails, the **freopen( )** function still continues to open the other file.

The **freopen( )** function returns a pointer to *stream* on success and a null pointer otherwise.

The main use of **freopen( )** is to redirect the system-defined files **stdin, stdout,** and **stderr** to some other file.

Related functions are **fopen( )** and **fclose( )**.

fscanf

```
#include <stdio.h>
int fscanf(FILE *stream, const char *format, ...);
```

The **fscanf( )** function works exactly like the **scanf( )** function, except that it reads the information from the stream specified by *stream* instead of **stdin**. See "**scanf( )**" for details.

The **fscanf( )** function returns the number of arguments actually assigned values. This number does not include skipped fields. A return value of **EOF** means that a failure occurred before the first assignment was made.

Related functions are **scanf( )** and **fprintf( )**.

fseek


```
#include <stdio.h>
int fseek(FILE *stream, long offset, int origin);
```

The **fseek( )** function sets the file position indicator associated with *stream* according to the values of *offset* and *origin*. Its purpose is to support random access I/O operations. The *offset* is the number of bytes from *origin* to seek to. The values for *origin* must be one of these macros (defined in STDIO.H):

Name	**Meaning**
SEEK_SET	Seek from start of file
SEEK_CUR	Seek from current location
SEEK_END	Seek from end of file

A return value of zero means that **fseek( )** succeeded. A nonzero value indicates failure.

You can use **fseek( )** to move the position indicator anywhere in the file, even beyond the end. However, it is an error to attempt to set the position indicator before the beginning of the file.

The **fseek( )** function clears the end-of-file flag associated with the specified stream. Furthermore, it nullifies any prior **ungetc( )** on the same stream (see "**ungetc( )**").

Related functions are **ftell( )**, **rewind( )**, **fopen( )**, **fgetpos( )**, and **fsetpos( )**.

fsetpos

```
#include <stdio.h>
int fsetpos(FILE *stream, const fpos_t *position);
```

The **fsetpos( )** function moves the file position indicator to the point specified by the object pointed to by *position*. This value must have been previously obtained through a call to **fgetpos( ).** The type **fpos_t** is defined in STDIO.H. After **fsetpos( )** is executed, the end-of-file indicator is reset. Also, any previous call to **ungetc( )** is nullified.

If **fsetpos( )** fails, it returns nonzero. If it is successful, it returns zero.

Related functions are **fgetpos( )**, **fseek( )**, and **ftell( )**.

ftell

```
#include <stdio.h>
long ftell(FILE *stream);
```

The **ftell( )** function returns the current value of the file position indicator for the specified *stream*. In the case of binary streams, the value is the number of bytes the indicator is from the beginning of the file. For text streams, the return value may not be meaningful except as an argument to **fseek( )** because of possible character translations, such as carriage return/linefeeds being substituted for newlines, which affect the apparent size of the file.

The **ftell( )** function returns −1 when an error occurs. If the stream is incapable of random seeks—if it is a modem, for instance—the return value is undefined.

Related functions are **fseek( )** and **fgetpos( )**.

fwrite

```
#include <stdio.h>
int fwrite(const void *buf, size_t size, size_t count,
           FILE *stream);
```

The **fwrite( )** function writes *count* number of objects, each object being *size* bytes in length, to the stream pointed to by *stream* from the character array pointed to by *buf*. The file position indicator is advanced by the number of characters written.

The **fwrite( )** function returns the number of items actually written, which, if the function is successful, will equal the number requested. If fewer items are written than are requested, an error has occurred. For text streams, various character translations can take place but will have no effect upon the return value.

Related functions are **fread( )**, **fscanf( )**, **getc( )**, and **fgetc( )**.

getc

```
#include <stdio.h>
int getc(FILE *stream);
```

The **getc( )** function returns the next character from the input *stream* at the current position and increments the file position indicator. The character is read as an **unsigned char** that is converted to an integer.

If the end of the file is reached, **getc( )** returns **EOF.** However, since **EOF** is a valid integer value, when working with binary files you must use **feof( )** to check for the end-of-file character. If **getc( )** encounters an error, **EOF** is also returned. If working with binary files, you must use **ferror( )** to check for file errors.

The functions **getc( )** and **fgetc( )** are identical, and in most implementations **getc( )** is simply defined as the macro shown here:

```
#define getc(fp) fgetc(fp)
```

This causes the **fgetc( )** function to be substituted for the **getc( )** macro.

Related functions are **fputc( )**, **fgetc( )**, **putc( )**, and **fopen( )**.

getchar

```
#include <stdio.h>
int getchar(void);
```

The **getchar( )** function returns the next character from **stdin**. The character is read as an **unsigned char** that is converted to an integer.

If the end of the file is reached, **getchar( )** returns **EOF**. However, since **EOF** is a valid integer value, when working with binary files you must use **feof( )** to check for end-of-file. If **getchar( )** encounters an error, **EOF** is also returned. If working with binary files, you must use **ferror( )** to check for file errors.

The **getchar( )** function is often implemented as a macro.

Related functions are **fputc( )**, **fgetc( )**, **putc( )**, and **fopen( )**.

gets

```
#include <stdio.h>
char *gets(char *str);
```

The **gets( )** function reads characters from **stdin** and places them into the character array pointed to by *str.* Characters are read until a newline or an **EOF** is received. The newline character is not made part of the string; instead, it is translated into a null to terminate the string.

If successful, **gets( )** returns *str;* a null pointer is returned upon failure. If a read error occurs, the contents of the array pointed to by *str* are indeterminate. Because a null pointer will be returned either when an error occurs or when the end of the file is reached, you should use **feof( )** or **ferror( )** to determine what has actually happened.

There is no way to limit the number of characters that **gets( )** will read, and it is therefore your job to make sure that the array pointed to by *str* will not be overrun. (See "Programming Tip," below.)

Related functions are **fputs( )**, **fgetc( )**, **fgets( )**, and **puts( )**.

Programming Tip

When using **gets( )** it is possible to overrun the array that is being used to receive the characters entered by the user because **gets( )** provides no bounds checking. One way around this problem is to use **fgets( )**, specifying **stdin** for the input stream. Since **fgets( )** requires you to specify a maximum length, it is possible to prevent an array overrun. The only trouble is that **fgets( )** does not remove the newline character that terminates input and **gets( )** does, so you will have to manually remove it, as shown in the following program:

```
#include <stdio.h>
#include <string.h>

int main(void)
{
  char str[10];
  int i;

  printf("Enter a string: ");
  fgets(str, 10, stdin);

  /* remove newline, if present */
  i = strlen(str)-1;
  if(str[i]=='\n') str[i] = '\0';

  printf("This is your string: %s", str);

  return 0;
}
```

Although using **fgets( )** requires a little more work, its advantage over **gets( )** is that you can prevent the input array from being overrun.

perror

```
#include <stdio.h>
void perror(const char *str);
```

The **perror( )** function maps the value of the global variable **errno** onto a string and writes that string to **stderr**. If the value of *str* is not null, the string is written first, followed by a colon and then the implementation-defined error message.

printf


```
#include <stdio.h>
int printf(const char *format, ...);
```

The **printf( )** function writes to **stdout** the arguments that make up the argument list as specified by the string pointed to by *format.*

The string pointed to by *format* consists of two types of items. The first type is made up of characters that will be printed on the screen. The second type contains format commands that define the way the arguments are displayed. A format command begins with a percent sign and is followed by the format code. There must be exactly the same number of arguments as there are format commands, and the format commands and the arguments are matched in order. For example, the following **printf( )** call displays "Hi c 10 there!":

```
printf("Hi %c %d %s", 'c', 10, "there!");
```

If there are insufficient arguments to match the format commands, the output is undefined. If there are more arguments than format commands, the remaining arguments are discarded. The format commands are shown here:

Code	**Format**
%c	Character
%d	Signed decimal integers
%i	Signed decimal integers
%e	Scientific notation (lowercase e)
%E	Scientific notation (uppercase E)

%f	Decimal floating point
%g	Uses %e or %f, whichever is shorter (if %e, uses lowercase e)
%G	Uses %E or %f, whichever is shorter (if %E, uses uppercase E)
%o	Unsigned octal
%s	String of characters
%u	Unsigned decimal integers
%x	Unsigned hexadecimal (lowercase letters)
%X	Unsigned hexadecimal (uppercase letters)
%p	Displays a pointer
%n	The associated argument shall be a pointer to an integer into which is placed the number of characters written so far.
%%	Prints a % sign

The **printf( )** function returns the number of characters actually printed. A negative return value indicates that an error has taken place.

The format commands can have modifiers that specify the field width, precision, and a left-justification flag. An integer placed between the % sign and the format command acts as a *minimum field-width specifier.* This pads the output with spaces or 0's to ensure that it is at least a certain minimum length. If the string or number is greater than that minimum, it will be printed in full, even if it overruns the minimum. The default padding is done with spaces. If you wish to pad with 0's, place a 0 before the field-width specifier. For example, **%05d** will pad a number of less than 5 digits with 0's so that its total length is 5.

The exact meaning of the *precision modifier* depends on the format code being modified. To add a precision modifier, place a decimal point followed by the precision after the field-width specifier. For **e**, **E**, and **f** formats, the precision modifier determines the number of decimal places printed. For example, **%10.4f** will display a number at least ten characters wide with four decimal places. When the precision modifier is applied to the **g** or **G** format code, it determines the maximum number of significant digits displayed. When applied to integers, the precision modifier specifies the minimum number of digits that will be displayed. Leading zeros are added, if necessary.

When the precision modifier is applied to strings, the number following the period specifies the maximum field length. For example, **%5.7s** will display a string that will be at least five characters long and will not exceed seven. If the string is longer than the maximum field width, the characters will be truncated off the end.

By default, all output is *right justified:* if the field width is larger than the data printed, the data will be placed on the right edge of the field. You can force the information to be left justified by placing a minus sign directly after the %. For example, **% – 10.2f** will left-justify a floating-point number with two decimal places in a ten-character field.

There are two format command modifiers that allow **printf( )** to display short and long integers. These modifiers can be applied to the **d**, **i**, **o**, **u**, and **x** type specifiers. The **l** modifier tells **printf( )** that a long data type follows. For example, **%ld** means that a long integer is to be displayed. The **h** modifier tells **printf( )** to display a short integer. Therefore, **%hu** indicates that the data is of type short unsigned integer.

The **l** modifier can also prefix the floating-point commands of **e**, **f**, and **g** and indicates that a **double** follows. To output a **long double**, use the **%L** prefix.

The **%n** command causes the number of characters that have been written at the time the **%n** is encountered to be placed in an integer variable that is pointed to by its corresponding argument. For example, this code fragment displays the number 14 after the line "this is a test":

```
int i;

printf("This is a test%n", &i);
printf("%d", i);
```

The # has a special meaning when used with some **printf( )** format codes. Preceding a **g**, **f**, or **e** code with a # ensures that the decimal point will be present, even if there are no decimal digits. If you precede the **x** format code with a #, the hexadecimal number will be printed with a **0x** prefix. If you precede the **o** format with a #, the octal value will be printed with a **0** prefix. The # cannot be applied to any other format specifiers.

The minimum field-width and precision specifiers can be provided by arguments to **printf( )** instead of by constants. To accomplish this, use an * as a placeholder. When the format string is scanned, **printf( )** will match each * to an argument in the order in which they occur.

Related functions are **scanf( )** and **fprintf( )**.

putc

```
#include <stdio.h>
int putc(int ch, FILE *stream);
```

The **putc( )** function writes the character contained in the least significant byte of *ch* to the output stream pointed to by *stream*. Because character arguments are elevated to integer at the time of the call, you can use character variables as arguments to **putc( )**.

The **putc( )** function returns the character written on success or **EOF** if an error occurs. If the output stream has been opened in binary mode, **EOF** is a valid value for *ch*. This means that you must use **ferror( )** to determine if an error has occurred.

Related functions are **fgetc( )**, **fputc( )**, **getchar( )**, and **putchar( )**.

putchar


```
#include <stdio.h>
int putchar(int ch);
```

The **putchar( )** function writes the character contained in the least significant byte of *ch* to **stdout**. It is functionally equivalent to **putc(ch, stdout)**. Because character arguments are elevated to integer at the time of the call, you can use character variables as arguments to **putchar( )**.

The **putchar( )** function returns the character written on success or **EOF** if an error occurs. If the output stream has been opened in binary mode, **EOF** is a valid value for *ch*. This means that you must use **ferror( )** to determine if an error has occurred.

A related function is **putc( )**.

puts

```
#include <stdio.h>
int puts(char *str);
```

The **puts( )** function writes the string pointed to by *str* to the standard output device. The null terminator is translated to a newline.

The **puts( )** function returns a nonnegative value if successful and an **EOF** upon failure.

Related functions are **putc( )**, **gets( )**, and **printf( )**.

remove

```
#include <stdio.h>
int remove(const char *fname);
```

The **remove( )** function erases the file specified by *fname.* It returns zero if the file was successfully deleted and nonzero if an error occurred.

A related function is **rename( )**.

rename

```
#include <stdio.h>
int rename(const char *oldfname, const char *newfname);
```

The **rename( )** function changes the name of the file specified by *oldfname* to *newfname.* The *newfname* must not match any existing directory entry.

The **rename( )** function returns zero if successful and nonzero if an error has occurred.

A related function is **remove( )**.

rewind

```
#include <stdio.h>
void rewind(FILE *stream);
```

The **rewind( )** function moves the file position indicator to the start of the specified stream. It also clears the end-of-file and error flags associated with *stream.* It has no return value.

A related function is **fseek( )**.

scanf

```
#include <stdio.h>
int scanf(const char *format, ...);
```

The **scanf( )** function is a general-purpose input routine that reads the stream **stdin** and stores the information in the variables pointed to in its argument list. It can read all the built-in data types and automatically convert them into the proper internal format.

The control string pointed to by *format* consists of three classifications of characters:

Format specifiers

Whitespace characters

Non-whitespace characters

The format specifiers are preceded by a % sign and tell **scanf( )** what type of data is to be read next. For example, **%s** reads a string while **%d** reads an integer. The **scanf( )** codes are matched in order with the variables receiving the input in the argument list. These codes are listed in the following table:

Code	**Meaning**
%c	Reads a single character
%d	Reads a decimal integer
%i	Reads an integer
%e	Reads a floating-point number
%f	Reads a floating-point number
%g	Reads a floating-point number
%o	Reads an octal number
%s	Reads a string
%x	Reads a hexadecimal number
%p	Reads a pointer
%n	Receives an integer value equal to the number of characters read so far
%u	Reads an unsigned integer
%[ ]	Scans for a set of characters
%%	Reads a percent sign

The format string is read left to right and the format codes are matched, in order, with the arguments that comprise the argument list.

A whitespace character in the format string causes **scanf( )** to skip over one or more whitespace characters in the input stream. A whitespace character is either a space, a tab character, or a newline. In essence, one whitespace character in the control string will cause **scanf( )** to read, but not store, any number (including zero) of whitespace characters up to the first non-whitespace character.

A non-whitespace character in the format string causes **scanf( )** to read and discard a matching character. For example, **%d,%d** causes **scanf( )** to first read an integer, then read and discard a comma, and finally read another integer. If the specified character is not found, **scanf( )** will terminate.

All the variables used to receive values through **scanf( )** must be passed by their addresses. This means that all arguments must be pointers to the variables receiving input.

The data items being input must be separated by spaces, tabs, or newlines. Punctuation such as commas, semicolons, and the like do not count as separators. This means that


```
scanf("%d%d", &r, &c);
```

will accept an input of **10 20** but will fail with **10,20**.

An * placed after the % and before the format code will read data of the specified type but suppress its assignment. Thus, the following command

```
scanf("%d%*c%d", &x, &y);
```

given the input **10/20**, will place the value 10 into **x**, discard the divide sign, and give **y** the value 20.

The format commands can specify a maximum field-length modifier. This is an integer number placed between the % and the format code that limits the number of characters read for any field. For example, if you wish to read no more than 20 characters into **address**, then you would write

```
scanf("%20s", address);
```

If the input stream had more than 20 characters, a subsequent call to input would begin where this call left off. Input for a field may terminate before the maximum field length is reached if a white space is encountered. In this case, **scanf( )** moves on to the next field.

Although spaces, tabs, and newlines are used as field separators, when reading a single character, these are read like any other character. For example, with an input stream of **x y**,

```
scanf("%c%c%c", &a, &b, &c);
```

will return with the character **x** in **a**, a space in **b**, and the character y in **c**.

Beware; any other characters in the control string—including spaces, tabs, and newlines—will be used to match and discard characters from the input stream. Any character that matches will be discarded. For example, given the input stream **10t20**,

```
scanf("%st%s", &x, &y);
```

will place 10 into **x** and 20 into **y**. The **t** is discarded because of the **t** in the control string.

Another feature of **scanf( )** is called a *scanset.* A scanset defines a set of characters that can be read by **scanf( )** and assigned to a corresponding character array. A scanset is defined by putting the characters you want to scan for inside square brackets. The beginning square bracket must be prefixed by a percent sign. For example, this scanset tells **scanf( )** to read only the characters A, B, and C:

```
%[ABC]
```

When a scanset is used, **scanf( )** continues to read characters and put them into the corresponding character array until a character that is not in the scanset is encountered. The corresponding variable must be a pointer to a character array. Upon return from **scanf( )**, the array will contain a null-terminated string comprised of the characters read.

You can specify an inverted set if the first character in the set is a ^. When the ^ is present, it instructs **scanf( )** to accept any character that *is not* defined by the scanset.

You can specify a range using a hyphen. For example, this tells **scanf( )** to accept the characters A through Z.

```
%[A-Z]
```

One important point to remember is that the scanset is case sensitive. Therefore, if you want to scan for both upper- and lowercase letters they must be specified individually.

The **scanf( )** function returns a number equal to the number of fields that were successfully assigned values. This number will not include fields that were read but not assigned because the * modifier was used to suppress the assignment. **EOF** is returned if an error occurs before the first field is assigned.

Related functions are **printf( )** and **fscanf( )**.

setbuf

```
#include <stdio.h>
void setbuf(FILE *stream, char *buf);
```

The **setbuf( )** function is used to either specify the buffer the specified stream will use or, if called with *buf* set to null, to turn off buffering. If a programmer-defined buffer is to be specified, it must be **BUFSIZ** characters long. **BUFSIZ** is defined in STDIO.H.

The **setbuf( )** function returns no value.

Related functions are **fopen( )**, **fclose( )**, and **setvbuf( )**.

setvbuf

```
#include <stdio.h>
int setvbuf(FILE *stream, char *buf, int mode, size_t size);
```

The **setvbuf( )** function allows the programmer to specify the buffer, its size, and its mode for the specified stream. The character array pointed to by *buf* is used as the stream buffer for I/O operations. The size of the buffer is set by *size*, and *mode* determines how buffering will be handled. If *buf* is null, **setvbuf( )** will allocate its own buffer.

The legal values of *mode* are **_IOFBF**, **_IONBF**, and **_IOLBF**. These are defined in STDIO.H. When *mode* is set to **_IOFBF**, full buffering will take place. If *mode* is **_IOLBF**, the stream will be line buffered, which means that the buffer will be flushed each time a newline character is written for output streams; for input streams, an input request reads all characters up to a newline. In either case, the buffer is also flushed when full. If mode is **_IONBF**, no buffering takes place.

The value of *size* must be greater than zero.

The **setvbuf( )** function returns zero on success, nonzero on failure.

A related function is **setbuf( )**.

sprintf

```
#include <stdio.h>
int sprintf(char *buf, const char *format, ...);
```

The **sprintf( )** function is identical to **printf( )** except that the output is put into the array pointed to by *buf* instead of being written to the console. See **printf( )** for details.

The return value is equal to the number of characters actually placed into the array.

Related functions are **printf( )** and **fsprintf( )**.

sscanf

```
#include <stdio.h>
int sscanf(const char *buf, const char *format, ...);
```

The **sscanf( )** function is identical to **scanf( )** except that data is read from the array pointed to by *buf* rather than from **stdin**. See "**scanf**" for details.

6

The return value is equal to the number of variables that were actually assigned values. This number does not include fields that were skipped through the use of the * format command modifier. A value of zero means that no fields were assigned, and **EOF** indicates that an error occurred prior to the first assignment.

Related functions are **scanf( )** and **fscanf( )**.

tmpfile

```
#include <stdio.h>
FILE *tmpfile(void);
```

The **tmpfile( )** function opens a temporary file for update and returns a pointer to the stream. The function automatically uses a unique filename to avoid conflicts with existing files.

The **tmpfile( )** function returns a null pointer on failure; otherwise it returns a pointer to the stream.

The temporary file created by **tmpfile( )** is automatically removed when the file is closed or when the program terminates.

A related function is **tmpnam( )**.

tmpnam

```
#include <stdio.h>
char *tmpnam(char *name);
```

The **tmpnam( )** function generates a unique filename and stores it in the array pointed to by *name*. The main purpose of **tmpnam( )** is to generate a temporary filename that is different from any other file in the current disk directory.

The function can be called up to **TMP_MAX** times. **TMP_MAX** is defined in STDIO.H, and it will be at least 25. Each time **tmpnam( )** is called, it will generate a new temporary filename.

A pointer to *name* is returned on success; otherwise a null pointer is returned.

A related function is **tmpfile( )**.

ungetc

```
#include <stdio.h>
int ungetc(int ch, FILE *stream);
```

The **ungetc( )** function returns the character specified by the low-order byte of *ch* to the input stream *stream*. This character will then be obtained by the next read operation on *stream*. A call to **fflush( )** or **fseek( )** undoes an **ungetc( )** operation and discards the character.

A one-character pushback is guaranteed; however, some implementations will accept more.

You cannot unget an **EOF.**

A call to **ungetc( )** clears the end-of-file flag associated with the specified stream. The value of the file position indicator for a text stream is undefined until all pushed-back characters are read, in which case it will be the same as it was prior to the first **ungetc( )** call. For binary streams, each **ungetc( )** call decrements the file position indicator.

The return value is equal to *ch* on success and **EOF** on failure.

A related function is **getc( )**.

vprintf, vfprintf, and vsprintf

```
#include <stdarg.h>
#include <stdio.h>
int vprintf(char *format, va_list arg_ptr);
int vfprintf(FILE *stream, const char *format, va_list
            arg_ptr);
int vsprintf(char *buf, char *format, va_list arg_ptr);
```

The functions **vprintf( )**, **vfprintf( )**, and **vsprintf( )** are functionally equivalent to **printf( )**, **fprintf( )**, and **sprintf( )**, respectively, except that the argument list has been replaced by a pointer to a list of arguments. This pointer must be of type **va_list** and is defined in STDARG.H.

Related functions are **va_arg( )**, **va_start( )**, and **va_end( )**.

Chapter 7—The C String and Character Functions

The C standard library has a rich and varied set of string- and character-handling functions. In C/C++, a string is a null-terminated array of characters. The string functions require the header file STRING.H to provide their prototypes. The character functions use CTYPE.H as their header file.

Because C/C++ has no bounds-checking on array operations, it is the programmer's responsibility to prevent an array overflow. Neglecting to do so may cause your program to crash.

In C/C++, a *printable character* is one that can be displayed on a terminal. These are usually the characters between a space (0x20) and tilde (0xFE). *Control characters* have values between 0 and 0x1F as well as DEL (0x7F).

For historical reasons, the arguments to the character functions are integers. However, only the low-order byte is used; the character functions automatically convert their arguments to **unsigned char**. You are free to call these functions with character arguments, because characters are automatically elevated to integers at the time of the call.

The header file STRING.H defines the **size_t** type, which is essentially the same as **unsigned**.

isalnum

```
#include <ctype.h>
int isalnum(int ch);
```

The **isalnum( )** function returns nonzero if its argument is either a letter of the alphabet or a digit. If the character is not alphanumeric, 0 is returned.

Related functions are **isalpha( )**, **iscntrl( )**, **isdigit( )**, **isgraph( )**, **isprint( )**, **ispunct( )**, and **isspace( )**.

isalpha

```
#include <ctype.h>
int isalpha(int ch);
```

The **isalpha( )** function returns nonzero if *ch* is a letter of the alphabet; otherwise, 0 is returned. What constitutes a letter of the alphabet varies from language to language. For English, these are the upper- and lowercase letters *A* through *Z*.

Related functions are **isalnum( )**, **iscntrl( )**, **isdigit( )**, **isgraph( )**, **isprint( )**, **ispunct( )**, and **isspace( )**.

iscntrl

```
#include <ctype.h>
int iscntrl(int ch);
```

The **iscntrl( )** function returns nonzero if *ch* is between 0 and 0x1F or is equal to 0x7F (DEL); otherwise, 0 is returned.

Related functions are **isalnum( )**, **isalpha( )**, **isdigit( )**, **isgraph( )**, **isprint( )**, **ispunct( )**, and **isspace( )**.

isdigit

```
#include <ctype.h>
int isdigit(int ch);
```

The **isdigit( )** function returns nonzero if *ch* is a digit, that is, 0 through 9. Otherwise, 0 is returned.

Related functions are **isalnum( )**, **isalpha( )**, **iscntrl( )**, **isgraph( )**, **isprint( )**, **ispunct( )**, and **isspace( )**.

isgraph

```
#include <ctype.h>
int isgraph(int ch);
```

The **isgraph( )** function returns nonzero if *ch* is any printable character other than a space; otherwise, 0 is returned. Printable characters are generally in the range 0x21 through 0x7E.

Related functions are **isalnum( )**, **isalpha( )**, **iscntrl( )**, **isdigit( )**, **isprint( )**, **ispunct( )**, and **isspace( )**.

islower

```
#include <ctype.h>
int islower(int ch);
```

The **islower( )** function returns nonzero if *ch* is a lowercase letter; otherwise, 0 is returned.

A related function is **isupper( )**.

isprint

```
#include <ctype.h>
int isprint(int ch);
```

The **isprint( )** function returns nonzero if *ch* is a printable character, including a space; otherwise, 0 is returned. Printable characters are often in the range 0x20 through 0x7E.

Related functions are **isalnum( )**, **isalpha( )**, **iscntrl( )**, **isdigit( )**, **isgraph( )**, **ispunct( )**, and **isspace( )**.

ispunct

```
#include <ctype.h>
int ispunct(int ch);
```

The **ispunct( )** function returns nonzero if *ch* is a punctuation character; otherwise, 0 is returned. The term *punctuation,* as defined by this function, includes all printing characters that are neither alphanumeric nor a space.

Related functions are **isalnum( )**, **isalpha( )**, **iscntrl( )**, **isdigit( )**, **isgraph( )**, **ispunct( )**, and **isspace( )**.

isspace

```
#include <ctype.h>
int isspace(int ch);
```

The **isspace( )** function returns nonzero if *ch* is either a space, horizontal tab, vertical tab, form feed, carriage return, or newline character; otherwise, 0 is returned.

Related functions are **isalnum( )**, **isalpha( )**, **iscntrl( )**, **isdigit( )**, **isgraph( )**, and **ispunct( )**.

isupper


```
#include <ctype.h>
int isupper(int ch);
```

The **isupper( )** function returns nonzero if *ch* is an uppercase letter; otherwise, 0 is returned.

A related function is **islower( )**.

isxdigit

```
#include <ctype.h>
int isxdigit(int ch);
```

The **isxdigit( )** function returns nonzero if *ch* is a hexadecimal digit; otherwise, 0 is returned. A hexadecimal digit will be in one of these ranges: A-F, a-f, or 0-9.

Related functions are **isalnum( )**, **isalpha( )**, **iscntrl( )**, **isdigit( )**, **isgraph( )**, **ispunct( )**, and **isspace( )**.

memchr

```
#include <string.h>
void *memchr(const void *buffer, int ch, size_t count);
```

The **memchr( )** function searches the array pointed to by *buffer* for the first occurrence of *ch* in the first *count* characters.

The **memchr( )** function returns a pointer to the first occurrence of *ch* in *buffer*, or it returns a null pointer if *ch* is not found.

Related functions are **memcpy( )** and **isspace( )**.

memcmp

```
#include <string.h>
int memcmp(const void *buf1, const void *buf2,
           size_t count);
```

The **memcmp( )** function compares the first *count* characters of the arrays pointed to by *buf1* and *buf2*.

The **memcmp( )** function returns an integer that is interpreted as indicated here:

Value	**Meaning**
Less than 0	*buf1* is less than *buf2*
0	*buf1* is equal to *buf2*
Greater than 0	*buf1* is greater than *buf2*

Related functions are **memchr( )**, **memcpy( )**, and **strcmp( )**.

memcpy

```
#include <string.h>
void *memcpy(void *to, const void *from, size_t count);
```

The **memcpy( )** function copies *count* characters from the array pointed to by *from* into the array pointed to by *to.* If the arrays overlap, the behavior of **memcopy( )** is undefined.

The **memcpy( )** function returns *to.*

A related function is **memmove( )**.

memmove

```
#include <string.h>
void *memmove(void *to, const void *from, size_t count);
```

The **memmove( )** function copies *count* characters from the array pointed to by *from* into the array pointed to by *to.* If the arrays overlap, the copy will take place correctly, placing the correct contents into *to* but leaving *from* modified.

The **memmove( )** function returns *to.*

A related function is **memcpy( )**.

memset

```
#include <string.h>
void *memset(void *buf, int ch, size_t count);
```

The **memset( )** function copies the low-order byte of *ch* into the first *count* characters of the array pointed to by *buf.* It returns *buf.*

The most common use of **memset( )** is to initialize a region of memory to some known value.

Related functions are **memcmp( )**, **memcpy( )**, and **memmove( )**.

strcat

```
#include <string.h>
char *strcat(char *str1, const char *str2);
```

The **strcat( )** function concatenates a copy of the string pointed to by *str2* to the string pointed to by *str1* and terminates *str1* with a null. The null terminator originally ending *str1* is overwritten by the first character of *str2.* The string *str2* is untouched by the operation. If the arrays overlap, the behavior of **strcat( )** is undefined.

The **strcat( )** function returns *str1.*

Remember, no bounds-checking takes place, so it is the programmer's responsibility to ensure that *str1* is large enough to hold both its original contents and also those of *str2.*

Related functions are **strchr( )**, **strcmp( )**, and **strcpy( )**.

strchr

```
#include <string.h>
char *strchr(const char *str, int ch);
```

The **strchr( )** function returns a pointer to the first occurrence of the low-order byte of *ch* in the string pointed to by *str.* If no match is found, a null pointer is returned.

Related functions are **strpbrk( )**, **strspn( )**, **strstr( )**, and **strtok( )**.

strcmp


```
#include <string.h>
int strcmp(const char *str1, const char *str2);
```

The **strcmp( )** function lexicographically compares two strings and returns an integer based on the outcome as shown here:

Value	**Meaning**
Less than 0	*str1* is less than *str2*
0	*str1* is equal to *str2*
Greater than 0	*str1* is greater than *str2*

Related functions are **strchr( )**, **strcpy( )**, and **strcmp( )**.

strcoll

```
#include <string.h>
int strcoll(const char *str1, const char *str2);
```

The **strcoll( )** function compares the string pointed to by *str1* with the one pointed to by *str2.* The comparison is performed in accordance to the locale specified using the **setlocale( )** function (see "**setlocale**" for details).

The **strcoll( )** function returns an integer that is interpreted as indicated here:

Value	**Meaning**
Less than 0	*str1* is less than *str2*
0	*str1* is equal to *str2*
Greater than 0	*str1* is greater than *str2*

Related functions are **memcmp( )** and **strcmp( )**.

strcpy

```
#include <string.h>
char *strcpy(char *str1, const char *str2);
```

The **strcpy( )** function copies the contents of the string pointed to by *str2* into the array pointed to by *str1*. *str2* must be a pointer to a null-terminated string. The **strcpy( )** function returns *str1*.

If *str1* and *str2* overlap, the behavior of **strcpy( )** is undefined.

Related functions are **memcpy( )**, **strchr( )**, **strcmp( )**, and **strncmp( )**.

strcspn

```
#include <string.h>
size_t strcspn(const char *str1, const char *str2);
```

The **strcspn( )** function returns the length of the initial substring of the string pointed to by *str1* that is made up of only those characters not contained in the string pointed to by *str2*. Stated differently, **strcspn( )** returns the index of the first character in the string pointed to by *str1* that matches any of the characters in the string pointed to by *str2*.

Related functions are **strrchr( )**, **strpbrk( )**, **strstr( )**, and **strtok( )**.

strerror

```
#include <string.h>
char *strerror(int errnum);
```

The **strerror( )** function returns a pointer to an implementation-defined string associated with the value of *errnum*. Under no circumstances should you modify the string.

strlen

```
#include <string.h>
size_t strlen(char *str);
```

The **strlen( )** function returns the length of the null-terminated string pointed to by *str*. The null is not counted.

Related functions are **memcpy( )**, **strchr( )**, **strcmp( )**, and **strncmp( )**.

strncat

```
#include <string.h>
char *strncat(char *str1, const char *str2, size_t count);
```

The **strncat( )** function concatenates not more that *count* characters of the string pointed to by *str2* to the string pointed to by *str1* and terminates *str1* with a null. The null terminator originally ending *str1* is overwritten by the first character of *str2*. The string *str2* is untouched by the operation. If the strings overlap, the behavior is undefined.

The **strncat( )** function returns *str1*.

Remember that no bounds-checking takes place, so it is the programmer's responsibility to ensure that *str1* is large enough to hold both its original contents and also those of *str2*.

Related functions are **strcat( )**, **strnchr( )**, **strncmp( )**, and **strncpy( )**.

strncmp

```
#include <string.h>
int strncmp(const char *str1, const char *str2,
            size_t count);
```

The **strncmp( )** function lexicographically compares not more than *count* characters from two null-terminated strings and returns an integer based on the outcome, as shown here:

Value	**Meaning**
Less than 0	*str1* is less than *str2*
0	*str1* is equal to *str2*
Greater than 0	*str1* is greater than *str2*

If there are less than *count* characters in either string, the comparison ends when the first null is encountered.

Related functions are **strcmp( )**, **strnchr( )**, and **strncpy( )**.

strncpy

```
#include <string.h>
char *strncpy(char *str1, const char *str2, size_t count);
```

The **strncpy( )** function is used to copy up to *count* characters from the string pointed to by *str2* into the string pointed to by *str1*. *str2* must be a pointer to a null-terminated string.

If *str1* and *str2* overlap, the behavior of **strncpy( )** is undefined.

If the string pointed to by *str2* has less than *count* characters, nulls will be appended to the end of *str1* until *count* characters have been copied.

Alternatively, if the string pointed to by *str2* is longer than *count* characters, the resultant string pointed to by *str1* will not be null-terminated.

The **strncpy( )** function returns *str1*.

Related functions are **memcpy( )**, **strchr( )**, **strncat( )**, and **strncmp( )**.

strpbrk

```
#include <string.h>
char *strpbrk(const char *str1, const char *str2);
```

The **strpbrk( )** function returns a pointer to the first character in the string pointed to by *str1* that matches any character in the string pointed to by *str2*. The null terminators are not included. If there are no matches, a null pointer is returned.

Related functions are **strspn( )**, **strrchr( )**, **strstr( )**, and **strtok( )**.

strrchr

```
#include <string.h>
char *strrchr(const char *str, int ch);
```

The **strrchr( )** function returns a pointer to the last occurrence of the low-order byte of *ch* in the string pointed to by *str.* If no match is found, a null pointer is returned.

Related functions are **strpbrk( )**, **strspn( )**, **strstr( )**, and **strtok( )**.

strspn

```
#include <string.h>
size_t strspn(const char *str1, const char *str2);
```

The **strspn( )** function returns the length of the initial substring of the string pointed to by *str1* that is made up of only those characters contained in the string pointed to by *str2.* Stated differently, **strspn( )** returns the index of the first character in the string pointed to by *str1* that does not match any of the characters in the string pointed to by *str2.*

Related functions are **strpbrk( )**, **strrchr( )**, **strstr( )**, and **strtok( )**.

strstr

```
#include <string.h>
char *strstr(const char *str1, const char *str2);
```

The **strstr( )** function returns a pointer to the first occurrence in the string pointed to by *str1* of the string pointed to by *str2.* It returns a null pointer if no match is found.

Related functions are **strchr( )**, **strcspn( )**, **strpbrk( )**, **strspn( )**, **strtok( )**, and **strrchr( )**.

strtok


```
#include <string.h>
char *strtok(char *str1, const char *str2);
```

The **strtok( )** function returns a pointer to the next token in the string pointed to by *str1*. The characters making up the string pointed to by *str2* are the delimiters that determine the token. A null pointer is returned when there is no token to return.

To tokenize a string, the first call to **strtok( )** must have *str1* point to the string being tokenized. Subsequent calls must use a null pointer for *str1*. In this way the entire string can be reduced to its tokens.

It is possible to use a different set of delimiters for each call to **strtok( )**.

Related functions are **strchr( )**, **strcspn( )**, **strpbrk( )**, **strrchr( )**, and **strspn( )**.

Programming Tip

The **strtok( )** function provides a means by which you can reduce a string to its constituent parts. For example, the following program tokenizes the string "One, two, and three."

```
#include <stdio.h>
#include <string.h>

int main(void)
{
  char *p;

  p = strtok("One, two, and three.", ",");
  printf(p);
  do {
    p = strtok(NULL, ",. ");
    if(p) printf("|%s", p);
  } while(p);
  return 0;
}
```

The output produced by this program is

One|two|and|three

Notice how **strtok( )** is first called with the string to be tokenized, but subsequent calls use **NULL** for the first argument. The **strtok( )** function maintains a pointer into the string being tokenized. When **strtok( )**'s first argument points to a string, this internal pointer is reset to the start of that string. When the first argument is **NULL**, **strtok( )** continues tokenizing the previous string from the point at which it left off, advancing the internal pointer as each token is obtained. This way, **strtok( )** can tokenize an entire string. Also notice how the string that defines the delimiters is changed between the first call and the subsequent calls. Each call can define the delimiters differently.

strxfrm

```
#include <string.h>
size_t strxfrm(char *str1, const char *str2, size_t count);
```

The **strxfrm( )** function transforms the first *count* characters of the string pointed to by *str2* so that it can be used by the **strcmp( )** function and puts the result into the string pointed to by *str1*. After the transformation, the outcome of a **strcmp( )** using *str1* and a **strcoll( )** using the original string pointed to by *str2* will be the same.

The **strxfrm( )** function returns the length of the transformed string.

A related function is **strcoll( )**.

tolower

```
#include <ctype.h>
int tolower(int ch);
```

The **tolower( )** function returns the lowercase equivalent of *ch* if *ch* is a letter; otherwise, *ch* is returned unchanged.

A related function is **toupper( )**.

toupper

```
#include <ctype.h>
int toupper(int ch);
```

The **toupper( )** function returns the uppercase equivalent of *ch* if *ch* is a letter; otherwise, *ch* is returned unchanged.

A related function is **tolower( )**.

Chapter 8—The C Mathematical Functions

The C standard library contains several mathematical functions, which fall into the following categories:

- Trigonometric functions
- Hyperbolic functions
- Exponential and logarithmic functions
- Miscellaneous functions

All of the math functions require the header file MATH.H. In addition to declaring the math functions, this header defines three macros called **EDOM**, **ERANGE**, and **HUGE_VAL**. If an argument to a math function is not in the domain for which it is defined, an implementation-defined value is returned, and the built-in global integer variable **errno** is set equal to **EDOM**. If a function produces a result that is too large to be represented by a **double**, an overflow occurs. This causes the function to return **HUGE_VAL**, and **errno** is set to **ERANGE**, indicating a range error. If an underflow happens, the function returns 0 and sets **errno** to **ERANGE**.

All angles are in radians.

acos

```
#include <math.h>
double acos(double arg);
```

The **acos( )** function returns the arc cosine of *arg*. The argument to **acos( )** must be in the range −1 to 1; otherwise, a domain error will occur.

Related functions are **asin( )**, **atan( )**, **atan2( )**, **sin( )**, **cos( )**, **tan( )**, **sinh( )**, **cosh( )**, and **tanh( )**.

asin

```
#include <math.h>
double asin(double arg);
```

The **asin( )** function returns the arc sine of *arg*. The argument to **asin( )** must be in the range −1 to 1; otherwise, a domain error will occur.

Related functions are **acos( )**, **atan( )**, **atan2( )**, **sin( )**, **cos( )**, **tan( )**, **sinh( )**, **cosh( )**, and **tanh( )**.

atan

```
#include <math.h>
double atan(double arg);
```

The **atan( )** function returns the arc tangent of *arg*.

Related functions are **asin( )**, **acos( )**, **atan2( )**, **tan( )**, **cos( )**, **sin( )**, **sinh( )**, **cosh( )**, and **tanh( )**.

atan2

```
#include <math.h>
double atan2(double y, double x);
```

The **atan2( )** function returns the arc tangent of *y/x*. It uses the signs of its arguments to compute the quadrant of the return value.

Related functions are **asin( )**, **acos( )**, **atan( )**, **tan( )**, **cos( )**, **sin( )**, **sinh( )**, **cosh( )**, and **tanh( )**.

ceil

```
#include <math.h>
double ceil(double num);
```

The **ceil( )** function returns the smallest integer (represented as a **double**) not less than *num*. For example, given 1.02, **ceil( )** would return 2.0. Given −1.02, **ceil( )** would return −1.

Related functions are **floor( )** and **fmod( )**.

cos

```
#include <math.h>
double cos(double arg);
```

The **cos( )** function returns the cosine of *arg*. The value of *arg* must be in radians.

Related functions are **asin( )**, **acos( )**, **atan2( )**, **atan( )**, **tan( )**, **sin( )**, **sinh( )**, **cos( )**, and **tanh( )**.

cosh

```
#include <math.h>
double cosh(double arg);
```

The **cosh( )** function returns the hyperbolic cosine of *arg*.

Related functions are **asin( )**, **acos( )**, **atan2( )**, **atan( )**, **tan( )**, **sin( )**, **cosh( )**, and **tanh( )**.

exp

```
#include <math.h>
double exp(double arg);
```

The **exp( )** function returns the natural logarithm *e* raised to the *arg* power.

A related function is **log( )**.

fabs

```
#include <math.h>
double fabs(double num);
```

The **fabs( )** function returns the absolute value of *num*.

A related function is **abs( )**.

floor

```
#include <math.h>
double floor(double num);
```

The **floor( )** function returns the largest integer (represented as a **double**) not greater than *num*. For example, given 1.02, **floor( )** would return 1.0. Given −1.02, **floor( )** would return −2.0.

Related functions are **fceil( )** and **fmod( )**.

fmod

```
#include <math.h>
double fmod(double x, double y);
```

The **fmod( )** function returns the remainder of x/y.

Related functions are **ceil( )**, **floor( )**, and **fabs( )**.

frexp

```
#include <math.h>
double frexp(double num, int *exp);
```

The **frexp( )** function decomposes the number *num* into a mantissa in the range 0.5 to less than 1, and an integer exponent such that $num = mantissa * 2^{exp}$. The mantissa is returned by the function, and the exponent is stored at the variable pointed to by *exp*.

A related function is **ldexp( )**.

ldexp

```
#include <math.h>
double ldexp(double num, int exp);
```

The **ldexp( )** returns the value of *num* $* 2^{exp}$. If overflow occurs, **HUGE_VAL** is returned.

Related functions are **frexp( )** and **modf( )**.

log

```
#include <math.h>
double log(double num);
```

The **log( )** function returns the natural logarithm for *num.* A domain error occurs if *num* is negative, and a range error occurs if the argument is 0.

A related function is **log10( )**.

log10

```
#include <math.h>
double log10(double num);
```

The **log10( )** function returns the base 10 logarithm for *num.* A domain error occurs if *num* is negative, and a range error occurs if the argument is 0.

A related function is **log( )**.

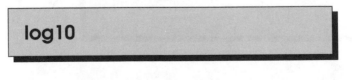

modf

```
#include <math.h>
double modf(double num, double *i);
```

The **modf( )** function decomposes *num* into its integer and fractional parts. It returns the fractional portion and places the integer part in the variable pointed to by *i*.

Related functions are **frexp( )** and **ldexp( )**.

pow

```
#include <math.h>
double pow(double base, double exp);
```

The **pow( )** function returns *base* raised to the *exp* power ($base^{exp}$). A domain error may occur if *base* is 0 and *exp* is less than or equal to 0. It will also happen if *base* is negative and *exp* is not an integer. An overflow produces a range error.

Related functions are **exp( ), log( )**, and **sqrt( )**.

sin

```
#include <math.h>
double sin(double arg);
```

The **sin( )** function returns the sine of *arg*. The value of *arg* must be in radians.

Related functions are **asin( )**, **acos( )**, **atan2( )**, **atan( )**, **tan( )**, **cos( )**, **sinh( )**, **cosh( )**, and **tanh( )**.

sinh

```
#include <math.h>
double sinh(double arg);
```

The **sinh( )** function returns the hyperbolic sine of *arg*.

Related functions are **asin( )**, **acos( )**, **atan2( )**, **atan( )**, **tan( )**, **cos( )**, **tanh( )**, **cosh( )**, and **sin( )**.

sqrt

```
#include <math.h>
double sqrt(double num);
```

The **sqrt( )** function returns the square root of *num*. If it is called with a negative argument, a domain error will occur.

Related functions are **exp( )**, **log( )**, and **pow( )**.

tan

```
#include <math.h>
double tan(double arg);
```

The **tan( )** function returns the tangent of *arg*. The value of *arg* must be in radians.

Related functions are **acos( )**, **asin( )**, **atan( )**, **atan2( )**, **cos( )**, **sin( )**, **sinh( )**, **cosh( )**, and **tanh( )**.

tanh

```
#include <math.h>
double tanh(double arg);
```

The **tanh( )** function returns the hyperbolic tangent of *arg*.

Related functions are **acos( )**, **asin( )**, **atan( )**, **atan2( )**, **cos( )**, **sin( )**, **cosh( )**, **sinh( )**, and **tan( )**.

Chapter 9—C's Time, Date, and Localization Functions

This section covers C's time and date functions and those functions that relate to the geographical location in which the computer is used.

C defines several functions that deal with the date and time of the system as well as elapsed time. These functions require the header file TIME.H. This header defines three time-related types: **clock_t**, **time_t**, and **tm**. The types **clock_t** and **time_t** are capable of representing the system time and date as some sort of integer. This is called the *calendar time*. The structure type **tm** holds the date and time broken down into its elements. The **tm** structure is defined as shown here:


```
struct tm {
  int tm_sec;   /* seconds, 0-61 */
  int tm_min;   /* minutes, 0-59 */
  int tm_hour;  /* hours, 0-23 */
  int tm_mday;  /* day of the month, 1-31 */
  int tm_mon;   /* months since Jan, 0-11 */
  int tm_year;  /* years from 1900 */
  int tm_wday;  /* days since Sunday, 0-6 */
  int tm_yday;  /* days since Jan 1, 0-365 */
  int tm_isdst  /* Daylight Saving Time indicator */
}
```

The value of **tm_isdst** will be positive if Daylight Saving Time is in effect, 0 if it is not in effect, and negative if there is no information available. This form of the time and date is called the *broken-down time*.

In addition, TIME.H defines the macro **CLOCKS_PER_SEC**, which is the number of system clock ticks per second.

The geographical location functions require the header file LOCALE.H.

Most C/C++ compilers will also supply additional time and date functions, so be sure to check the user's manual for your compiler for these types of functions.

asctime

```
#include <time.h>
char *asctime(const struct tm *ptr);
```

The **asctime( )** function returns a pointer to a string that converts the information stored in the structure pointed to by *ptr* into the following form.

day month date hours:minutes:seconds year\ *n*\ *0*

Here is an example:

```
Wed Jun 19 12:05:34 1999
```

The structure pointer passed to **asctime( )** is generally obtained from either **localtime( )** or **gmtime( )**.

The buffer used by **asctime( )** to hold the formatted output string is a statically allocated character array and is overwritten each time the function is called. If you wish to save the contents of the string, you must copy it elsewhere.

Related functions are **localtime( )**, **gmtime( )**, **time( )**, and **ctime( )**.

clock

```
#include <time.h>
clock_t clock(void);
```

The **clock( )** function returns a value that approximates the amount of time the calling program has been running. To transform this value into seconds, divide it by **CLOCKS_PER_SEC**. A value of −1 is returned if the time is not available.

Related functions are **time( )**, **asctime( )**, and **ctime( )**.

ctime

```
#include <time.h>
char *ctime(const time_t *time);
```

The **ctime( )** function returns a pointer to a string of the form

day month date hours:minutes:seconds year\n\0

given a pointer to the calendar time. The calendar time is generally obtained through a call to **time( )**.

The buffer used by **ctime( )** to hold the formatted output string is a statically allocated character array and is overwritten each time the function is called. If you wish to save the contents of the string, it is necessary to copy it elsewhere.

Related functions are **localtime( )**, **gmtime( )**, **time( )**, and **asctime( )**.

difftime

```
#include <time.h>
double difftime(time_t time2, time_t time1);
```

The **difftime( )** function returns the difference, in seconds, between *time1* and *time2*. That is, it returns *time2* − *time1*.

Related functions are **localtime( )**, **gmtime( )**, **time( )**, **asctime( )**.

gmtime

```
#include <time.h>
struct tm *gmtime(const time_t *time);
```

The **gmtime( )** function returns a pointer to the broken-down form of *time* in the form of a **tm** structure. The time is represented in Coordinated Universal Time (UTC), which is essentially Greenwich mean time. The *time* value is generally obtained through a call to **time( )**. If the system does not support Coordinated Universal Time, a **NULL** is returned.

The structure used by **gmtime( )** to hold the broken-down time is statically allocated and is overwritten each time the function is called. If you wish to save the contents of the structure, you must copy it elsewhere.

Related functions are **localtime( )**, **time( )**, and **asctime( )**.

localeconv

```
#include <locale.h>
struct lconv *localeconv(void);
```

The **localeconv( )** function returns a pointer to a structure of type **lconv**, which contains various country-specific environmental information relating to the way numbers are formatted. The

lconv structure is organized as shown here:

```
struct lconv {
  char *decimal_point;      /* decimal point character
                               for nonmonetary values */
  char *thousands_sep;      /* thousands separator
                               for nonmonetary values */
  char *grouping;           /* specifies grouping for
                               nonmonetary values */
  char int_curr_symbol;     /* international
                               currency symbol */
  char *currency_symbol;    /* local currency symbol */
  char *mon_decimal_point; /* decimal point character for
                               monetary values */
  char *mon_thousands_sep; /* thousands separator
                               for monetary values */
  char *mon_grouping;       /* specifies grouping for
                               monetary values */
  char *positive_sign;      /* positive value indicator
                               for monetary values */
  char *negative_sign;      /* negative value indicator
                               for monetary values */
  char int_frac_digits,     /* number of digits
                               displayed to the right
                               of the decimal point
                               for monetary values
                               displayed using international
                               format */
  char frac_digits;         /* number of digits
                               displayed to the right
                               of the decimal point
                               for monetary values
                               displayed using local
                               format */
  char p_cs_precedes;       /* 1 if currency symbol
                               precedes positive value,
                               0 if currency symbol
                               follows value */
  char p_sep_by_space;      /* 1 if currency symbol is
                               separated from
                               value by a space, 0
                               otherwise */
```

9

```
  char n_cs_precedes;       /* 1 if currency symbol
                               precedes a negative value,
                               0 if currency symbol
                               follows value */
  char n_sep_by_space;      /* 1 if currency symbol is
                               separated from a negative
                               value by a space, 0 if
                               currency symbol follows
                               value */
  char p_sign_posn;         /* indicates position of
                               positive value symbol */
  char n_sign_posn;         /* indicates position of
                               negative value symbol */
}
```

The **localeconv( )** function returns a pointer to the **lconv** structure. You must not alter the contents of this structure. Refer to your compiler's documentation for implementation-specific information relating to the **lconv** structure.

A related function is **setlocale( )**.

localtime

```
#include <time.h>
struct tm *localtime(const time_t *time);
```

The **localtime( )** function returns a pointer to the broken-down form of *time* in the form of a **tm** structure. The time is represented in local time. The *time* value is generally obtained through a call to **time( )**.

The structure used by **localtime( )** to hold the broken-down time is statically allocated and is overwritten each time the function is called. If you wish to save the contents of the structure, you must copy it elsewhere.

Related functions are **gmtime( )**, **time( )**, and **asctime( )**.

mktime

```
#include <time.h>
time_t mktime(struct tm *time);
```

The **mktime( )** function returns the calendar-time equivalent of the broken-down time found in the structure pointed to by *time*. The elements **tm_wday** and **tm_yday** are set by the function, so they need not be defined at the time of the call.

If **mktime( )** cannot represent the information as a valid calendar time, −1 is returned.

Related functions are **time( )**, **gmtime( )**, **asctime( )**, and **ctime( )**.

Programming Tip

The **mktime( )** function is especially useful when you want to know on what day of the week a given date falls. For example, what day of the week is January 12, 2012? To find out, call the **mktime( )** function with that date and then examine the **tm_wday** member of the **tm** structure after the function returns. It will contain the day of the week. The following program demonstrates this method.

```
/* Find day of week for January 12, 2012. */
#include <stdio.h>
#include <time.h>

char day[][20]= {
  "Sunday",
  "Monday",
```

```
  "Tuesday",
  "Wednesday",
  "Thursday",
  "Friday",
  "Saturday"
};

int main(void)
{
  struct tm t;

  t.tm_mday = 12;
  t.tm_mon = 0;
  t.tm_year = 112;
  t.tm_hour = 0;
  t.tm_min = 0;
  t.tm_sec = 0;
  t.tm_isdst = 0;

  mktime(&t); /* fill in day of week */

  printf("Day of week is %s.\n", day[t.tm_wday]);

  return 0;
}
```

When this program is run, **mktime( )** automatically computes the day of the week, which is Thursday in this case. Since the return value of **mktime( )** is not needed, it is simply ignored.

setlocale

```
#include <locale.h>
char *setlocale(int type, const char *locale);
```

The **setlocale( )** function allows certain parameters that are sensitive to the geographical location of a program's execution to be queried or set. For example, in Europe, the comma is used in place of the decimal point.

If *locale* is null, **setlocale( )** returns a pointer to the current localization string. Otherwise, **setlocale( )** attempts to use the specified localization string to set the locale parameters as specified by *type*.

At the time of the call, *type* must be one of the following macros:

LC_ALL
LC_COLLATE
LC_CTYPE
LC_MONETARY
LC_NUMERIC
LC_TIME

LC_ALL refers to all localization categories. **LC_COLLATE** affects the operation of the **strcoll( )** function. **LC_CTYPE** alters the way the character functions work. **LC_MONETARY** determines the monetary format. **LC_NUMERIC** changes the decimal-point character for formatted input/output functions. Finally, **LC_TIME** determines the behavior of the **strftime( )** function.

The ANSI C standard defines two possible strings for *locale*. The first is "C", which specifies a minimal environment for C compilation. The second is " ", the null string, which specifies the implementation-defined default environment. All other values for *locale* are implementation-defined and will affect portability.

The **setlocale( )** function returns a pointer to a string associated with the *type* parameter.

Related functions are **localeconv( )**, **time( )**, **strcoll( )**, and **strftime( )**.

strftime

```
#include <time.h>
size_t strftime(char *str, size_t maxsize, const
                char *fmt, const struct tm *time);
```

The **strftime( )** function places time and date information, along with other information, into the string pointed to by *str* according to the format commands found in the string pointed to by *fmt* and using the broken-down time *time*. A maximum of *maxsize* characters will be placed into *str*.

The **strftime( )** function works a little like **sprintf( )** in that it recognizes a set of format commands that begin with the percent sign (%) and it places its formatted output into a string. The format commands are used to specify the exact way various time and date information is represented in *str*. Any other characters found in the format string are placed into *str* unchanged. The time and date displayed are in local time. The format commands are shown in the following table. Notice that many of the commands are case sensitive.

Command	Replaced By
%a	Abbreviated weekday name
%A	Full weekday name
%b	Abbreviated month name
%B	Full month name
%c	Standard date and time string
%d	Day of month as a decimal (1-31)
%H	Hour (0-23)
%I	Hour (1-12)
%j	Day of year as a decimal (1-366)
%m	Month as decimal (1-12)

Command	Replaced By
%M	Minute as decimal (0-59)
%p	Locale's equivalent of AM or PM
%S	Second as decimal (0-61)
%U	Week of year, Sunday being first day (0-53)
%w	Weekday as a decimal (0-6, Sunday being 0)
%W	Week of year, Monday being first day (0-53)
%x	Standard date string
%X	Standard time string
%y	Year in decimal without century (0-99)
%Y	Year including century as decimal
%Z	Time zone name
%%	The percent sign

The **strftime( )** function returns the number of characters placed in the string pointed to by *str* or 0 if an error occurs.

Related functions are **time( )**, **localtime( )**, and **gmtime( )**.

time

```
#include <time.h>
time_t time(time_t *time);
```

The **time( )** function returns the current calendar time of the system. If the system has no time, −1 is returned.

The **time( )** function can be called either with a null pointer or with a pointer to a variable of type **time_t**. If the latter is used, the variable will also be assigned the calendar time.

Related functions are **localtime( )**, **gmtime( )**, **strftime( )**, and **ctime( )**.

Chapter 10—The C Dynamic Allocation Functions

This section describes C's dynamic allocation system. At the core are the functions **malloc( )** and **free( )**. Each time **malloc( )** is called, a portion of the remaining free memory is allocated. Each time **free( )** is called, memory is returned to the system. The region of free memory from which memory is allocated is called the *heap*. The prototypes for the dynamic allocation functions are in STDLIB.H.

All C/C++ compilers will include at least these four dynamic allocation functions: **calloc( )**, **malloc( )**, **free( )**, and **realloc( )**. However, your compiler will almost certainly contain several variants on these functions to accommodate various options and environmental differences. You will want to refer to your compiler's documentation.

While C++ supports the dynamic allocation functions described here, you will typically not use them in a C++ program. The reason for this is that C++ provides special dynamic allocation operators called **new** and **delete**. There are several advantages to using C++'s dynamic allocation operators. First, **new** automatically allocates the correct amount of memory for the type of data being allocated. Second, it returns the correct type of pointer to that memory. Third, both **new** and **delete** can be overloaded. Since **new** and **delete** have advantages over C's dynamic allocation functions, their use is recommended for C++ programs. (For a discussion of **new** and **delete**, see Chapter 5.)

calloc

```
#include <stdlib.h>
void *calloc(size_t num, size_t size);
```

The **calloc( )** function allocates memory the size of which is equal to *num* * *size*. That is, **calloc( )** allocates sufficient memory for an array of *num* objects of size *size*.

The **calloc( )** function returns a pointer to the first byte of the allocated region. If there is not enough memory to satisfy the request, a null pointer is returned. It is always important to verify that the return value is not a null pointer before attempting to use it.

Related functions are **free( )**, **malloc( )**, and **realloc( )**.

free

```
#include <stdlib.h>
void free(void *ptr);
```

The **free( )** function returns the memory pointed to by *ptr* to the heap. This makes the memory available for future allocation.

It is imperative that **free( )** only be called with a pointer that was previously allocated using one of the dynamic allocation system's functions (either **malloc( )** or **calloc( )**). Using an invalid pointer in the call most likely will destroy the memory management mechanism and cause a system crash.

Related functions are **calloc( )**, **malloc( )**, and **realloc( )**.

malloc

```
#include <stdlib.h>
void *malloc(size_t size);
```

The **malloc( )** function returns a pointer to the first byte of a region of memory of size *size* that has been allocated from the heap. If there is insufficient memory in the heap to satisfy the request, **malloc( )** returns a null pointer. It is always important to verify that the return value is not a null pointer before attempting to use it. Attempting to use a null pointer will usually result in a system crash.

Related functions are **free( )**, **realloc( )**, and **calloc( )**.

Programming Tip

If you are writing 16-bit programs for the 8086 family of processors (such as the 80486 or Pentium), then your compiler will provide additional allocation functions that accommodate the segmented memory model used by these processors when operating in 16-bit mode. For example, there will be functions that allocate memory from the FAR heap (the heap that is outside the default data segment), that can allocate pointers to memory that is larger than one segment, and that free such memory.

realloc

```
#include <stdlib.h>
void *realloc(void *ptr, size_t size);
```

The **realloc( )** function changes the size of the previously allocated memory pointed to by *ptr* to that specified by *size*. The value of *size* may be greater or less than the original. A pointer to the memory block is returned because it may be necessary for **realloc( )** to move the block in order to increase its size. If this occurs, the contents of the old block are copied into the new block—no information is lost.

If *ptr* is null, **realloc( )** simply allocates *size* bytes of memory and returns a pointer to it. If *size* is zero, the memory pointed to by *ptr* is freed.

If there is not enough free memory in the heap to allocate *size* bytes, a null pointer is returned and the original block is left unchanged.

Related functions are **free( )**, **malloc( )**, and **calloc( )**.

Chapter 11—Miscellaneous C Functions

The functions discussed in this chapter don't easily fit into any other category. They include various conversions, variable-length argument processing, sorting and searching, and random number generation.

Many of the functions covered here require the use of the header STDLIB.H. In this header are defined the two types, **div_t** and **ldiv_t**, which are the types of the values returned by **div( )** and **ldiv( )**, respectively. Also defined is the type **size_t**, which is the unsigned value returned by **sizeof**. These macros are also defined:

Macro	**Meaning**
NULL	A null pointer
RAND_MAX	The maximum value that can be returned by the **rand( )** function
EXIT_FAILURE	The value returned to the calling process if program termination is unsuccessful
EXIT_SUCCESS	The value returned to the calling process if program termination is successful

If a function requires a different header file than STDLIB.H, that function description will discuss it.

abort

```
#include <stdlib.h>
void abort(void);
```

The **abort( )** function causes immediate abnormal termination of a program. Generally, no files are flushed. In environments that support it, **abort( )** will return an implementation-defined value to the calling process (usually the operating system) indicating failure.

Related functions are **exit( )** and **atexit( )**.

abs

```
#include <stdlib.h>
int abs(int num);
```

The **abs( )** function returns the absolute value of the integer *num*.

A related function is **labs( )**.

assert

```
#include <assert.h>
void assert(int exp);
```

The **assert( )** macro, defined in its header ASSERT.H, writes error information to **stderr** and then aborts program execution if the expression *exp* evaluates to 0. Otherwise, **assert( )** does nothing. Although the exact output is implementation-defined, many compilers use a message similar to this:

Assertion failed: <*expression*>, file <*file*>, line <*linenum*>

The **assert( )** macro is generally used to help verify that a program is operating correctly, with the expression being devised in such a way that it evaluates to true only when no errors have taken place.

It is not necessary to remove the **assert( )** statements from the source code once a program is debugged because if the macro **NDEBUG** is defined (as anything), the **assert( )** macros will be ignored.

A related function is **abort( )**.

atexit

```
#include <stdlib.h>
int atexit(void (*func)(void));
```

The **atexit( )** function causes the function pointed to by *func* to be called upon normal program termination. The **atexit( )** function returns 0 if the function is successfully registered as a termination function, and nonzero otherwise.

At least 32 termination functions can be established, and they will be called in the reverse order of their establishment.

Related functions are **exit( )** and **abort( )**.

atof

```
#include <stdlib.h>
double atof(const char *str);
```

The **atof( )** function converts the string pointed to by *str* into a **double** value. The string must contain a valid floating-point number. If this is not the case, the returned value is undefined.

The number can be terminated by any character that cannot be part of a valid floating-point number. This includes whitespace characters, punctuation (other than periods), and characters other than "E" or "e". This means that if **atof( )** is called with "100.00HELLO", the value 100.00 will be returned.

Related functions are **atoi( )** and **atol( )**.

atoi

```
#include <stdlib.h>
int atoi(const char *str);
```

The **atoi( )** function converts the string pointed to by *str* into an **int** value. The string must contain a valid integer number. If this is not the case, the returned value is undefined; however, most implementations will return 0.

The number can be terminated by any character that cannot be part of an integer number. This includes whitespace characters, punctuation, and characters. This means that if **atoi( )** is called with "123.23", the integer value 123 will be returned, and the ".23" is ignored.

Related functions are **atof( )** and **atol( )**.

atol

```
#include <stdlib.h>
long atol(const char * str);
```

The **atol( )** function converts the string pointed to by *str* into a **long** value. The string must contain a valid long integer number.

If this is not the case, the returned value is undefined; however, most implementations will return 0.

The number can be terminated by any character that cannot be part of an integer number. This includes whitespace characters, punctuation, and characters. This means that if **atol( )** is called with "123.23", the long integer value 123L will be returned, and the ".23" is ignored.

Related functions are **atof( )** and **atoi( )**.

bsearch

```
#include <stdlib.h>
void *bsearch(const void *key, const void *buf,
              size_t num, size_t size, int
              (*compare)(const void *, const void *));
```

The **bsearch( )** function performs a binary search on the sorted array pointed to by *buf* and returns a pointer to the first member that matches the key pointed to by *key*. The number of elements in the array is specified by *num*, and the size (in bytes) of each element is described by *size*.

The function pointed to by *compare* is used to compare an element of the array with the key. The form of the *compare* function must be as follows:

int *func_name*(const void **arg1*, const void **arg2*);

It must return values as described in the following table:

Comparison	**Value Returned**
arg1 is less than *arg2*	Less than 0
arg1 is equal to *arg2*	0
arg1 is greater than *arg2*	Greater than 0

11

The array must be sorted in ascending order with the lowest address containing the lowest element.

If the array does not contain the key, a null pointer is returned.

A related function is **qsort( )**.

div

```
#include <stdlib.h>
div_t div(int numerator, int denominator);
```

The **div( )** function returns the quotient and the remainder of the operation *numerator/denominator* in a structure of type **div_t**.

The structure type **div_t** is defined in STDLIB.H and will have at least these two fields:

```
int quot; /* the quotient */
int rem;  /* the remainder */
```

A related function is **ldiv( )**.

exit

```
#include <stdlib.h>
void exit(int exit_code);
```

The **exit( )** function causes immediate, normal termination of a program.

The value of *exit_code* is passed to the calling process, usually the operating system, if the environment supports it. By convention, if the value of *exit_code* is 0, or **EXIT_SUCCESS**, normal program termination is assumed. A nonzero value, or **EXIT_FAILURE**, is used to indicate an implementation-defined error.

Related functions are **atexit( )** and **abort( )**.

getenv

```
#include <stdlib.h>
char *getenv(const char *name);
```

The **getenv( )** function returns a pointer to environmental information associated with the string pointed to by *name* in the implementation-defined environmental information table.

The environment of a program can include such things as path names and devices online. The exact nature of this data is implementation-defined. You will need to refer to your compiler's user manual for details.

If a call is made to **getenv( )** with an argument that does not match any of the environment data, a null pointer is returned.

A related function is **system( )**.

labs

```
#include <stdlib.h>
long labs(long num);
```

The **labs( )** function returns the absolute value of *num*.

A related function is **abs( )**.

ldiv

```
#include <stdlib.h>
ldiv_t ldiv(long numerator, long denominator);
```

The **ldiv( )** function returns the quotient and the remainder of the operation *numerator/denominator*.

The structure type **ldiv_t** is defined in STDLIB.H and will have at least these two fields:

```
long quot; /* the quotient */
long rem;  /* the remainder */
```

A related function is **div( )**.

longjmp

```
#include <setjmp.h>
void longjmp(jmp_buf envbuf, int status);
```

The **longjmp( )** function causes program execution to resume at the point of the last call to **setjmp( )**. These two functions provide a means of jumping between functions. Notice that the header SETJMP.H is required.

The **longjmp( )** function operates by resetting the stack to the state as described in *envbuf*, which must have been set by a prior call to **setjmp( )**. This causes program execution to resume at the statement following the **setjmp( )** invocation. That is, the computer is "tricked" into thinking that it never left the function that called **setjmp( )**. (As a somewhat graphic explanation, the **longjmp( )** function "warps" across time and (memory) space to a previous point in your program without having to perform the normal function return process.)

The buffer *evnbuf* is of type **jmp_buf**, which is defined in the header SETJMP.H. The buffer must have been set through a call to **setjmp( )** prior to calling **longjmp( )**.

The value of *status* becomes the return value of **setjmp( )** and can be interrogated to determine where the long jump came from. The only value that is not allowed is 0.

By far the most common use of **longjmp( )** is to return from a deeply nested set of routines when an error occurs.

A related function is **setjmp( )**.

qsort

```
#include <stdlib.h>
void qsort(void *buf, size_t num, size_t size,
           int (*compare) (const void *,
                           const void *));
```


The **qsort( )** function sorts the array pointed to by *buf* using a Quicksort (developed by C.A.R. Hoare). The Quicksort is considered the best general-purpose sorting algorithm. Upon termination, the array will be sorted. The number of elements in the array is specified by *num*, and the size (in bytes) of each element is described by *size*.

The function pointed to by *compare* is used to compare two elements of the array. The form of the *compare* function must be as follows:

int *func_name*(const void **arg1*, const void **arg2*);

It must return values as described here:

Comparison	Value Returned
arg1 is less than *arg2*	Less than 0
arg1 is equal to *arg2*	0
arg1 is greater than *arg2*	Greater than 0

The array is sorted in ascending order, with the lowest address containing the lowest element.

A related function is **bsearch( )**.

Programming Tip

When using **qsort( )**, if you want to sort an array in descending order (that is, high to low), simply reverse the conditions used by the comparison function. That is, have the comparison function return the following values:

Comparison	Value Returned
arg1 is less than *arg2*	Greater than 0
arg1 is equal to *arg2*	0
arg1 is greater than *arg2*	Less than 0

Also, if you want to use the **bsearch( )** function on an array that is sorted in descending order, you will need to use a reversed comparison function.

raise

```
#include <signal.h>
int raise(int signal);
```

The **raise( )** function sends the signal specified by *signal* to the executing program. It returns 0 if successful, nonzero otherwise. It uses the header file SIGNAL.H.

The following signals are defined by the ANSI C standard. Of course, your compiler is free to provide additional signals.

Macro	**Meaning**
SIGABRT	Termination error
SIGFPE	Floating-point error
SIGILL	Bad instruction
SIGINT	User pressed Ctrl-C
SIGSEGV	Illegal memory access
SIGTERM	Terminate program

A related function is **signal( )**.

rand


```
#include <stdlib.h>
int rand(void);
```

The **rand( )** function generates a sequence of pseudorandom numbers. Each time it is called, an integer between 0 and **RAND_MAX** is returned.

A related function is **srand( )**.

setjmp

```
#include <setjmp.h>
int setjmp(jmp_buf envbuf);
```

The **setjmp( )** function saves the contents of the system stack in the buffer *envbuf* for later use by **longjmp( )**. It uses the header file SETJMP.H.

The **setjmp( )** function returns 0 upon invocation. However, **longjmp( )** passes an argument to **setjmp( )** when it executes, and it is this value (always nonzero) that will appear to be the value of **setjmp( )** after a call to **longjmp( )** has occurred. (See "**longjmp**", earlier in this chapter, for additional information.)

A related function is **longjmp( )**.

signal

```
#include <signal.h>
void (*signal(int signal, void (*func) (int))) (int);
```

The **signal( )** function registers the function pointed to by *func* as a handler for the signal specified by *signal*. That is, the function pointed to by *func* will be called when *signal* is received by your program.

The value of *func* can be the address of a signal handler function or one of the following macros, defined in SIGNAL.H:

Macro	Meaning
SIG_DFL	Use default signal handling
SIG_IGN	Ignore the signal

If a function address is used, the specified handler will be executed when its signal is received.

On success, **signal( )** returns the address of the previously defined function for the specified signal. On error, **SIG_ERR** (defined in SIGNAL.H) is returned.

A related function is **raise( )**.

srand

```
#include <stdlib.h>
void srand(unsigned seed);
```

The **srand( )** function is used to set a starting point for the sequence generated by **rand( )**. (The **rand( )** function returns pseudorandom numbers.)

srand( ) is generally used to allow multiple program runs to use different sequences of pseudorandom numbers by specifying different starting points. Conversely, you can also use **srand( )** to generate the same pseudorandom sequence over and over again by calling it with the same seed before starting each sequence.

A related function is **rand( )**.

strtod

```
#include <stdlib.h>
double strtod(const char *start, char **end);
```

The **strtod( )** function converts the string representation of a number stored in the string pointed to by *start* into a **double** and returns the result.

The **strtod( )** function works as follows. First, any whitespace characters in the string pointed to by *start* are stripped. Next, each character in the number is read. Any character that cannot be part of a floating-point number will cause this process to stop. This includes whitespace characters, punctuation (other than periods), and characters other than "E" or "e". Finally, *end* is set to point to the remainder, if any, of the original string. This means that if **strtod( )** is called with "100.00 Pliers", the value 100.00 will be returned, and *end* will point to the space that precedes "Pliers".

If no conversion takes place, 0 is returned. If overflow occurs, **strtod( )** returns either **HUGE_VAL** or −**HUGE_VAL** (indicating positive or negative overflow), and the global variable **errno** is set to **ERANGE**, indicating a range error. If underflow occurs, then 0 is returned, and the global variable **errno** is set to **ERANGE**.

A related function is **atof( )**.

strtol

```
#include <stdlib.h>
long strtol(const char *start, char **end,
            int radix);
```

The **strtol( )** function converts the string representation of a number stored in the string pointed to by *start* into a **long** and returns the result. The base of the number is determined by *radix*. If *radix* is 0, the base is determined by rules that govern constant specification. If the radix is other than 0, it must be in the range 2 through 36.

The **strtol( )** function works as follows. First, any whitespace characters in the string pointed to by *start* are stripped. Next, each character in the number is read. Any character that cannot be part of a long integer number will cause this process to stop. This includes whitespace characters, punctuation, and characters. Finally, *end* is set to point to the remainder, if any, of the original string. This means that if **strtol( )** is called with "100 Pliers", the value 100L will be returned, and *end* will point to the space that precedes "Pliers".

If the result cannot be represented by a long integer, **strtol( )** returns either **LONG_MAX** or **LONG_MIN**, and the global **errno** is set to **ERANGE**, indicating a range error. If no conversion takes place, 0 is returned.

A related function is **atol( )**.

strtoul

```
#include <stdlib.h>
unsigned long strtoul(const char *start, char **end,
                      int radix);
```


The **strtoul( )** function converts the string representation of a number stored in the string pointed to by *start* into an **unsigned long** and returns the result. The base of the number is determined by *radix*. If *radix* is 0, the base is determined by rules that govern constant specification. If the radix is specified, it must be in the range 2 through 36.

The **strtoul( )** function works as follows. First, any whitespace characters in the string pointed to by *start* are stripped. Next, each character in the number is read. Any character that cannot be part of an unsigned long integer number will cause this process to stop. This includes whitespace characters, punctuation, and characters. Finally, *end* is set to point to the remainder, if any, of the original string. This means that if **strtoul( )** is called with "100 Pliers", the value 100L will be returned, and *end* will point to the space that precedes "Pliers".

If the result cannot be represented by an unsigned long integer, **strtoul( )** returns **ULONG_MAX** and the global variable **errno** is set to **ERANGE**, indicating a range error. If no conversion takes place, 0 is returned.

A related function is **strtol( )**.

system

```
#include <stdlib.h>
int system(const char *str);
```

The **system( )** function passes the string pointed to by *str* as a command to the command processor of the operating system.

If **system( )** is called with a null pointer, it will return nonzero if a command processor is present, 0 otherwise. (Some C/C++ code will be executed in dedicated systems that do not have operating systems and command processors, so you may not be able to assume that a command processor is present.) The return value of **system( )** is implementation-defined. However, generally it will return 0 if the command was successfully executed, and nonzero otherwise.

A related function is **exit( )**.

va_arg, va_start, AND va_end

```
#include <stdarg.h>
type va_arg(va_list argptr, type);
void va_end(va_list argptr);
void va_start(va_list argptr, last_parm);
```

The **va_arg( )**, **va_start( )**, and **va_end( )** macros work together to allow a variable number of arguments to be passed to a function. The most common example of a function that takes a variable number of arguments is **printf( )**. The type **va_list** is defined by STDARG.H.

The general procedure for creating a function that can take a variable number of arguments is as follows. The function must have at least one known parameter, but can have more, prior to the variable parameter list. The rightmost known parameter is called the *last_parm*. The name of *last_parm* is used as the second parameter in a call to **va_start( )**. Before any of the variable-length parameters can be accessed, the argument pointer *argptr* must be initialized through a call to **va_start( )**. After that, parameters are returned via calls to **va_arg( )**, with *type* being the type of the next parameter. Finally, once all the parameters have been read and prior to returning from the function, a call to **va_end( )** must be made to ensure that the stack is properly restored. If **va_end( )** is not called, a program crash is very likely.

A related function is **vprintf( )**.

Programming Tip

The proper use of **va_start( ), va_end( )**, and **va_arg( )** is best illustrated with an example. This program uses **sum_series( )** to return the sum of a series of numbers. The first argument contains a count of the number of arguments to follow. In this example, the first five elements of the following series are summed:

$$\frac{1}{2} + \frac{1}{4} + \frac{1}{8} + \frac{1}{16} \; . \; . \; . + \frac{1}{2^n}$$

The output displayed is "0.968750".

```
/* Variable length argument example - sum a series.*/

#include <stdio.h>
#include <stdarg.h>

double sum_series(int, ...);

int main(void)
{
  double d;

  d = sum_series(5, 0.5, 0.25, 0.125,
                 0.0625, 0.03125);

  printf("Sum of series is %f\n",d);

  return 0;
}

double sum_series(int num, ...)
{
  double sum = 0.0, t;
  va_list argptr;

  /* initialize argptr */
  va_start(argptr, num);

  /* sum the series */
  for(; num; num--) {
   t = va_arg(argptr, double);
   sum += t;
  }

  /* do orderly shutdown */
  va_end(argptr);
  return sum;
}
```

Chapter 12—The Old-Style C++ I/O System

Because C++ includes the entire C library, it supports the use of C's I/O system. However, C++ also defines its own class-based, object-oriented I/O system, which is referred to as the *iostream library.* When writing C++ programs you will usually want to use the iostream library rather than C-based I/O.

At the time of this writing there are two versions of the iostream library in use: the older one, based on the original specifications for C++, and the newer one, defined by the ANSI C++ standards committee. Today, most C++ compilers support both the old- and new-style iostream libraries. And fortunately, for the most part, they both work the same way. If you know how to use one, you can easily use the other. However, there are several important differences between the two.

First, the original iostream classes were defined in the global namespace. The new standard iostream library is contained in the **std** namespace.

Second, the new iostream library is defined using a complex, interrelated set of template classes and functions. The old-style library uses a less-complicated, nontemplatized class hierarchy. Fortunately, the names of the classes that you will use in your programs remain the same.

Third, the new iostream library defines many new data types.

Fourth, to use the old library, you need to include .H header files, such as IOSTREAM.H. These header files define the old-style iostream classes and put them into the global name space. By contrast, to use the new, standard iostream library, include the new style header **<iostream>** in your program.

Because of the differences between the old and the new iostream libraries, they will be described separately in this reference. This section describes the old-style library. The next chapter describes the new, standard iostream library.

THE BASIC STREAM CLASSES

The old-style iostream library uses the header file IOSTREAM.H. This file defines the foundational class hierarchy that supports I/O operations. If you will be performing file I/O, then you will also need to include FSTREAM.H. To use array-based I/O you will need to include STRSTREA.H.

The lowest-level class is called **streambuf**. This class provides the basic input and output operations. It is used primarily as a base class for other classes. Unless you are deriving your own I/O classes, you will not use **streambuf** directly.

The class **ios** is the base class of the class hierarchy that you will typically use when using the C++ I/O system. It provides formatting, error checking, and status information. From **ios** are derived several classes—sometimes through intermediary classes. The classes derived either directly or indirectly from **ios** that you will typically use are listed here:

Class	Purpose
istream	General input
ostream	General output
iostream	General input/output
ifstream	File input
ofstream	File output
fstream	File input/output
istrstream	Array-based input
ostrstream	Array-based output
strstream	Array-based input/output

C++'S PREDEFINED STREAMS

When a C++ program begins execution, four built-in streams are automatically opened. They are listed here:

Stream	Meaning	Default Device
cin	Standard input	Keyboard
cout	Standard output	Screen
cerr	Standard error output	Screen
clog	Buffered version of cerr	Screen

By default, the standard streams are used to communicate with the console. However, in environments that support I/O redirection (such as DOS, UNIX, and Windows), the standard streams can be redirected to other devices or files.

THE FORMAT FLAGS

In the C++ I/O system, each stream has associated with it a set of format flags that control the way information is formatted by a stream. In **ios** are defined the following enumerated values. These values are used to set or clear the format flags:

adjustfield	hex	scientific	stdio
basefield	internal	showbase	unitbuf
dec	left	showpoint	uppercase
fixed	oct	showpos	
floatfield	right	skipws	

Since these flags are defined within the **ios** class you will need to explicitly specify this when using them in a program. For example, to refer to **left** you will write **ios::left**.

When the **skipws** flag is set, leading whitespace characters (spaces, tabs, and newlines) are discarded when performing input on a stream. When **skipws** is cleared, whitespace characters are not discarded.

When the **left** flag is set, output is left-justified. When **right** is set, output is right-justified. When the **internal** flag is set, a numeric value is padded to fill a field by inserting spaces between any sign or base character. If none of these flags is set, output is right-justified by default.

By default, numeric values are output in decimal. However, it is possible to change the number base. Setting the **oct** flag causes output to be displayed in octal. Setting the **hex** flag causes output to be displayed in hexadecimal. To return output to decimal, set the **dec** flag.

Setting **showbase** causes the base of numeric values to be shown. For example, if the conversion base is hexadecimal, the value 1F will be displayed as 0x1F.

By default, when scientific notation is displayed, the "e" is in lowercase. Also, when a hexadecimal value is displayed, the "x" is in lowercase. When **uppercase** is set, these characters are displayed in uppercase.

Setting **showpos** causes a leading plus sign to be displayed before positive values.

Setting **showpoint** causes a decimal point and trailing zeros to be displayed for all floating-point output—whether needed or not.

By setting the **scientific** flag, floating-point numeric values are displayed using scientific notation. When **fixed** is set, floating-point values are displayed using normal notation. When neither flag is set, the compiler chooses an appropriate method.

When **unitbuf** is set, the buffer is flushed after each insertion operation.

When **stdio** is set, **stdout** and **stderr** are flushed after each output.

Since it is common to refer to the **oct**, **dec**, and **hex** fields, they can be collectively referred to as **ios::basefield**. Similarly, the **left**, **right**, and **internal** fields can be referred to as **ios::adjustfield**. Finally, the **scientific** and **fixed** fields can be referenced as **ios::floatfield**.

The format flags are typically stored in a **long** integer and can be set by various member functions of the **ios** class.

The I/O Manipulators

In addition to setting or clearing the format flags directly, there is another way to alter the format parameters of a stream. This second way is through the use of special functions called *manipulators,* which can be included in an I/O expression. The manipulators defined by the old-style iostream library are shown in the following table:

Manipulator	**Purpose**	**Input/Output**
dec	Use decimal integers	Input/Output
endl	Output a newline character and flush the stream	Output
ends	Output a null	Output
flush	Flush a stream	Output
hex	Use hexadecimal integers	Input/Output
oct	Use octal integers	Input/Output
resetiosflags (long *f*)	Turn off the flags specified in *f*	Input/Output
setbase(int *base*)	Set the number base to *base*	Output
setfill(int *ch*)	Set the fill character to *ch*	Output
setiosflags (long *f*)	Turn on the flags specified in *f*	Input/Output
setprecision (int *p*)	Set the number of digits of precision	Output
setw(int *w*)	Set the field width to *w*	Output
ws	Skip leading white space	Input

To access manipulators that take parameters, such as **setw( )**, you must include IOMANIP.H in your program.

Programming Tip

As you know, there are two flavors of manipulators: those without parameters and those with parameters. While the creation of parameterized manipulators is beyond the scope of this book, it is quite easy to create your own parameterless manipulators.

All parameterless output manipulators have this skeleton:

```
ostream &manip-name(ostream &stream)
{
  // your code here
  return stream;
}
```

Here, *manip-name* is the name of the manipulator. Notice that a reference to a stream of type **ostream** is returned. This is necessary if a manipulator is to be used as part of a larger I/O expression. It is important to understand that even though the manipulator has as its single argument a reference to the stream upon which it is operating, no argument is used when the manipulator is inserted in an output operation.

All parameterless input manipulators have this skeleton:

```
istream &manip-name(istream &stream)
{
  // your code here
  return stream;
}
```

An input manipulator receives a reference to the stream for which it was invoked. This stream must be returned by the manipulator.

Here is an example of a simple output manipulator called **setup( )**. It turns on left-justification, sets the field width to 10, and specifies the dollar sign as the fill character.

```
#include <iostream.h>
#include <iomanip.h>

ostream &setup(ostream &stream)
{
  stream.setf(ios::left);
  stream << setw(10) << setfill('$');
  return stream;
}

int main()
{
  cout << 10 << " " << setup << 10;

  return 0;
}
```

Remember: It is crucial that your manipulator return *stream*. If this is not done, your manipulator cannot be used in a series of input or output operations.

THE OLD-STYLE IOSTREAM FUNCTIONS

The most commonly used of the old-style iostream functions are described next.

bad

```
#include <iostream.h>
int bad() const;
```

The **bad( )** function is a member of **ios**.

The **bad( )** function returns nonzero if a fatal I/O error has occurred in the associated stream; otherwise, 0 is returned.

A related function is **good( )**.

clear

```
#include <iostream.h>
void clear(int flags = 0);
```

The **clear( )** function is a member of **ios**.

The **clear( )** function clears the status flags associated with a stream. If *flags* is 0 (as it is by default), then all error flags are cleared (reset to 0). Otherwise, the status flags will be set to whatever value is specified in *flags.*

A related function is **rdstate( )**.

eatwhite

```
#include <iostream.h>
void eatwhite();
```

The **eatwhite( )** function is a member of **istream**.

The **eatwhite( )** function reads and discards all leading white space from the associated input stream and advances the get pointer to the first non-whitespace character.

A related function is **ignore( )**.

eof

```
#include <iostream.h>
int eof() const;
```

The **eof( )** function is a member of **ios**.

The **eof( )** function returns nonzero when the end of the associated input file has been encountered; otherwise, it returns 0.

Related functions are **bad( )**, **fail( )**, **good( )**, **rdstate( )**, and **clear( )**.

fail

```
#include <iostream.h>
int fail() const;
```

The **fail( )** function is a member of **ios**.

The **fail( )** function returns nonzero if an I/O error has occurred in the associated stream. Otherwise, it returns 0.

Related functions are **good( )**, **eof( )**, **bad( )**, **clear( )**, and **rdstate( )**.

fill

```
#include <iostream.h>
char fill() const;
char fill(char ch);
```


The **fill( )** function is a member of **ios**.

By default, when a field needs to be filled, it is filled with spaces. However, you can change the fill character using the **fill( )** function, specifying the new fill character in *ch*. The old fill character is returned.

To obtain the current fill character, use the first form of **fill( )**, which returns the current fill character.

Related functions are **precision( )** and **width( )**.

flags

```
#include <iostream.h>
long flags() const;
long flags(long f);
```

The **flags( )** function is a member of **ios**.

The first form of **flags( )** simply returns the current format flags settings of the associated stream.

The second form of **flags( )** sets all format flags associated with a stream as specified by *f*. This version also returns the previous settings.

Related functions are **unsetf( )** and **setf( )**.

flush

```
#include <iostream.h>
ostream &flush();
```

The **flush( )** function is a member of **ostream**.

The **flush( )** function causes the buffer connected to the associated output stream to be physically written to the device. The function returns a reference to its associated stream.

Related functions are **put( )** and **write( )**.

fstream, ifstream, and ofstream

```
#include <fstream.h>
fstream();
fstream(const char *filename, int mode,
        int access=filebuf::openprot);
fstream(int fd);
fstream(int fd, char *buf, int size);
```

```
ifstream();
ifstream(const char *filename, int mode=ios::in,
         int access=filebuf::openprot);
ifstream(int fd);
ifstream(int fd, char *buf, int size);

ofstream();
ofstream(const char *filename, int mode=ios::out,
         int access=filebuf::openprot);
ofstream(int fd);
ofstream(int fd, char *buf, int size);
```

fstream( ), **ifstream( )**, and **ofstream( )** are the constructors of the **fstream**, **ifstream**, and **ofstream** classes, respectively.

The versions of **fstream( )**, **ifstream( )**, and **ofstream( )** that take no parameters create a stream that is not associated with any file. This stream can then be linked to a file using **open( )**.

The versions of **fstream( )**, **ifstream( )**, and **ofstream( )** that take a filename for their first parameters are the most commonly used in application programs. Although it is entirely proper to open a file using the **open( )** function, most of the time you will not do so because these **ifstream**, **ofstream**, and **fstream** constructor functions automatically open the file when the stream is created. The constructor functions have the same parameters and defaults as the **open( )** function. (See "**open**" for details.) Therefore, the most common way you will see a file opened is shown in this example:

```
ifstream mystream("myfile");
```

If for some reason the file cannot be opened, the value of the associated stream variable will be 0. Therefore, whether you use a constructor function to open the file or an explicit call to **open( )**, you will want to confirm that the file has actually been opened by testing the value of the stream.

The versions of **fstream( )**, **ifstream( )**, and **ofstream( )** that take only one parameter, an already-valid file descriptor, create a

12

stream and then associate that stream with the file descriptor specified in *fd*.

The versions of **fstream( )**, **ifstream( )**, and **ofstream( )** that take a file descriptor, a pointer to a buffer, and a size create a stream and associate it with the file descriptor specified in *fd*. *buf* must be a pointer to memory that will serve as a buffer, and *size* specifies the length of the buffer in bytes. (If *buf* is null and/or if *size* is 0, no buffering takes place.)

Related functions are **close( )** and **open( )**.

gcount

```
#include <iostream.h>
int gcount() const;
```

The **gcount( )** function is a member of **istream**.

The **gcount( )** function returns the number of characters read by the last input operation.

Related functions are **get( )**, **getline( )**, and **read( )**.

get

```
#include <iostream.h>
int get();
istream &get(char &ch):
istream &get(char *buf, int num, char delim = '\n');
istream &get(streambuf &buf, char delim = '\n');
```

The **get( )** function is a member of **istream**.

In general, **get( )** reads characters from an input stream. The parameterless form of **get( )** reads a single character from the associated stream and returns that value.

The form of **get( )** that takes a single character reference reads a character from the associated stream and puts that value in *ch*. It returns a reference to the stream. (Note that *ch* can also be of type **unsigned char** * or **signed char** *.)

The form of **get( )** that takes three parameters reads characters into the array pointed to by *buf* until either *num* characters have been read or the character specified by *delim* has been encountered. The array pointed to by *buf* will be null terminated by **get( )**. If no *delim* parameter is specified, by default a newline character acts as a delimiter. If the delimiter character is encountered in the input stream it *is not* extracted. Instead, it remains in the stream until the next input operation. This function returns a reference to the stream. (Note that *buf* can also be of type **unsigned char** * or **signed char** *.)

The form of **get( )** that takes two parameters reads characters from the input stream into the **streambuf** (or derived) object. Characters are read until the specified delimiter is encountered. It returns a reference to the stream.

Related functions are **put( )**, **read( )**, and **getline( )**.

getline

```
#include <iostream.h>
istream &getline(char *buf, int num, char delim = '\n');
```


The **getline( )** function is a member of **istream**.

The **getline( )** function reads characters into the array pointed to by *buf* until either *num* characters have been read or the character specified by *delim* has been encountered. The array pointed to by *buf* will be null terminated by **getline( )**. If no *delim* parameter is specified, by default a newline character acts as a delimiter. If the delimiter character is encountered in the input stream it is extracted, but is not put into *buf*. This function returns a reference to the stream. (Note that *buf* can also be of type **unsigned char** * or **signed char** *.)

Related functions are **get( )** and **read( )**.

good

```
#include <iostream.h>
int good() const;
```

The **good( )** function is a member of **ios**.

The **good( )** function returns nonzero if no I/O errors have occurred in the associated stream; otherwise, it returns 0.

Related functions are **bad( )**, **fail( )**, **eof( )**, **clear( )**, and **rdstate( )**.

ignore

```
#include <iostream.h>
istream &ignore(int num = 1, int delim = EOF);
```

The **ignore( )** function is a member of **istream**.

You can use the **ignore( )** member function to read and discard characters from the input stream. It reads and discards characters until either *num* characters have been ignored (1 by default) or the character specified by *delim* is encountered (**EOF** by default). If the delimiting character is encountered, it is removed from the input stream. The function returns a reference to the stream.

Related functions are **get( )** and **getline( )**.

open

```
#include <fstream.h>
 void open(const char *filename, int mode,
           int access=filebuf::openprot);
```

The **open( )** function is a member of **fstream**, **ifstream**, and **ofstream**.

A file is associated with a stream by using the **open( )** function. Here, *filename* is the name of the file, which may include a path specifier. The value of *mode* determines how the file is opened. It must be one (or more) of these values:

ios::app

ios::ate

ios::binary

ios::in

ios::nocreate

ios::noreplace

ios::out

ios::trunc

You can combine two or more of these values by ORing them together.

Including **ios::app** causes all output to that file to be appended to the end. This value can only be used with files capable of output. Including **ios::ate** causes a seek to the end of the file to occur when the file is opened. Although **ios::ate** causes a seek to the end-of-file, I/O operations can still occur anywhere within the file.

The **ios::binary** value causes the file to be opened for binary I/O operations. By default, files are opened in text mode.

The **ios::in** value specifies that the file is capable of input. The **ios::out** value specifies that the file is capable of output. However, creating a stream using **ifstream** implies input, and creating a stream using **ofstream** implies output, so in these cases it is unnecessary to supply these values.

The **ios::trunc** value causes the contents of a preexisting file by the same name to be destroyed and the file to be truncated to zero length.

Including **ios::nocreate** causes the **open( )** function to fail if the file does not already exist. The **ios::noreplace** value causes the **open( )** function to fail if the file already exists and **ios::ate** or **ios::app** is not also specified.

The value of *access* determines how the file can be accessed. Its default value is **filebuf::openprot** (**filebuf** is a base class of the file classes), which means a normal file. Check your compiler's documentation for other legal values of *access.*

When opening a file, both *mode* and *access* will default. When opening an input file, *mode* will default to **ios::in**. When opening an output file, *mode* will default to **ios::out**. In either case, the default for *access* is a normal file. For example, this fragment opens a file called TEST for output:

```
out.open("test"); // defaults to output and normal file
```

To open a stream for input and output, you must specify both the **ios::in** and the **ios::out** *mode* values, as shown here:

```
mystream.open("test", ios::in | ios::out);
```

No default value for *mode* is supplied when opening read/write files.

In all cases, if **open( )** fails, the stream will be 0. Therefore, before using a file, you should test to make sure that the open operation succeeded.

Related functions are **close( )**, **fstream( )**, **ifstream( )**, and **ofstream( )**.

Programming Tip

To read from or write to a text file you simply use the << and >> operators with the stream you opened. For example, the following program writes an integer, a floating-point value, and a string to a file called TEST and then reads them back.

```
#include <iostream.h>
#include <fstream.h>

int main()
{
  ofstream out("test");
  if(!out) {
    cout << "Cannot open file.\n";
    return 1;
    }

  // output data
  out << 10 << " " << 123.23 << "\n";
  out << "This is a short text file.\n";
  out.close();

  // now, read it back
  char ch;
  int i;
  float f;
  char str[80];

  ifstream in("test");
  if(!in) {
    cout << "Cannot open file.\n";
    return 1;
  }

  in >> i;
  in >> f;
  in >> ch;
  in >> str;
```

```
  cout << "Here is the data: ";
  cout << i << " " << f << " " << ch << "\n";
  cout << str;

  in.close();

  return 0;
}
```

When reading text files using the >> operator, keep in mind that certain character translations occur. For example, whitespace characters are omitted. If you want to prevent any character translations, you must open the file for binary I/O and use C++'s binary I/O functions.

peek

```
#include <iostream.h>
int peek();
```

The **peek( )** function is a member of **istream**.

The **peek( )** function returns the next character in the stream or **EOF** if the end of the file is encountered. It does not, under any circumstances, remove the character from the stream.

A related function is **get( )**.

precision

```
#include <iostream.h>
int precision() const;
int precision(int p);
```

The **precision( )** function is a member of **ios**.

By default, six digits of precision are displayed when floating-point values are output. However, using the second form of **precision( )** you can set this number to the value specified in *p*. The original value is returned.

The first version of **precision( )** returns the current value.

Related functions are **width( )** and **fill( )**.

put

```
#include <iostream.h>
ostream &put(char ch);
```

The **put( )** function is a member of **ostream**.

The **put( )** function writes *ch* to the associated output stream. It returns a reference to the stream.

Related functions are **write( )** and **get( )**.

putback

```
#include <iostream.h>
istream &putback(char ch);
```


The **putback( )** function is a member of **istream**.

The **putback( )** function returns *ch* to the associated input stream.

Note: ch *must be the last character read from that stream.*

A related function is **peek( )**.

rdstate

```
#include <iostream.h>
int rdstate() const;
```

The **rdstate( )** function is a member of **ios**.

The **rdstate( )** function returns the status of the associated stream. The C++ I/O system maintains status information about the outcome of each I/O operation relative to each active stream. The current state of the I/O system is held in an integer, in which the following flags are encoded:

Name	Meaning
ios::goodbit	No errors occurred
ios::eofbit	End-of-file is encountered
ios::failbit	A nonfatal I/O error has occurred
ios::badbit	A fatal I/O error has occurred

These flags are enumerated inside **ios**.

rdstate( ) returns 0 (**ios::goodbit**) when no error has occurred; otherwise, an error bit has been set.

Related functions are **eof( )**, **good( )**, **bad( )**, **clear( )**, and **fail( )**.

read

```
#include <iostream.h>
istream &read(char *buf, int num);
```

The **read( )** function is a member of **istream**.

The **read( )** function reads *num* bytes from the associated input stream and puts them in the buffer pointed to by *buf* (note that *buf* can also be of type **unsigned char *** or **signed char ***). If the end of the file is reached before *num* characters have been read, **read( )** simply stops, and the buffer contains as many characters as were available. (See "**gcount**".) **read( )** returns a reference to the stream.

Related functions are **gcount( )**, **get( )**, **getline( )**, and **write( )**.

seekg and seekp

```
#include <iostream.h>
istream &seekg(streamoff offset, ios::seek_dir origin)
istream &seekg(streampos position);

ostream &seekp(streamoff offset, ios::seek_dir origin);
ostream &seekp(streampos position);
```

The **seekg( )** function is a member of **istream**, and the **seekp( )** function is a member of **ostream**.

In C++'s I/O system, you perform random access using the **seekg( )** and **seekp( )** functions. To this end, the C++ I/O system manages two pointers associated with a file. One is the *get pointer,* which specifies where in the file the next input operation will occur. The other is the *put pointer,* which specifies where in the file the next output operation will occur. Each time an input or an output operation takes place, the appropriate pointer is automatically sequentially advanced. However, using the **seekg( )** and **seekp( )** functions, it is possible to access the file in a nonsequential fashion.

The two-parameter version of **seekg( )** moves the get pointer *offset* number of bytes from the location specified by *origin.* The two-parameter version of **seekp( )** moves the put pointer *offset* number of bytes from the location specified by *origin.* The *offset* parameter is of type **streamoff**, which is defined in IOSTREAM.H. A **streamoff** object is capable of containing the largest valid value that *offset* can have.

The *origin* parameter is of type **ios::seek_dir** and is an enumeration that has these values:

ios::beg	Seek from beginning
ios::cur	Seek from current position
ios::end	Seek from end

The single-parameter versions of **seekg( )** and **seekp( )** move the file pointers to the location specified by *position.* This value must have been previously obtained using a call to either **tellg( )** or **tellp( )**, respectively. **streampos** is a type defined in IOSTREAM.H that is capable of containing the largest valid value that *position* can have. These functions return a reference to the associated stream.

Related functions are **tellg( )** and **tellp( )**.

setf

```
#include <iostream.h>
long setf(long flags);
long setf(long flags1, long flags2);
```

The **setf( )** function is a member of **ios**.

The first version of **setf( )** turns on the format flags specified by *flags.* (All other flags are unaffected.) For example, to turn on the **showpos** flag, you can use this statement:

```
stream.setf(ios::showpos);
```

Here, *stream* is the stream you wish to affect.

It is important to understand that a call to **setf( )** is done relative to a specific stream. There is no concept of calling **setf( )** by itself. Put differently, there is no concept in C++ of global format status. Each stream maintains its own format status information individually.

When you want to set more than one flag, you can OR together the values of the flags you want set.

The second version of **setf( )** affects only the flags that are set in *flags2.* The corresponding flags are first reset and then set according to the flags specified by *flags1.* It is important to understand that even if *flags1* contains other set flags, only those specified by *flags2* will be affected.

Both versions of **setf( )** return the previous settings of the format flags associated with the stream.

Related functions are **unsetf( )** and **flags( )**.

setmode

```
#include <fstream.h>
int setmode(int mode = filebuf::text);
```

The **setmode( )** function is a member of **ofstream** and **ifstream**.

Tho **setmode( )** function sets the mode of the associated stream to either binary or text. (Text is the default.) The valid values for *mode* are **filebuf::text** and **filebuf::binary**.

The function returns the previous mode setting or −1 if an error occurs.

A related function is **open( )**.

str

```
#include <strstrea.h>
char *str();
```

The **str( )** function is a member of **strstream**.

The **str( )** function "freezes" a dynamically allocated input array and returns a pointer to it. Once a dynamic array is frozen, it cannot be used for output again. Therefore, you will not want to freeze the array until you are through outputting characters to it.

Note: This function is for use with array-based I/O.

Related functions are **strstream( )**, **istrstream( )**, and **ostrstream( )**.

strstream, istrstream, and ostrstream

```
#include <strstrea.h>
strstream();
strstream(char *buf, int size, int mode);

istrstream(const char *buf);
istrstream(const char *buf, int size);

ostrstream();
ostrstream(char *buf, int size, int mode=ios::out)
```

The **strstream** constructor is a member of **strstream**, the **istrstream( )** constructor is a member of **istrstream**, and the **ostrstream( )** constructor is a member of **ostrstream**.

These constructors are used to create array-based streams that support C++'s array-based I/O functions.

For **ostrstream( ),** *buf* is a pointer to the array that collects characters written to the stream. The size of the array is passed in the *size* parameter. By default, the stream is opened for normal output, but you can specify a different mode using the *mode* parameter. The legal values for *mode* are the same as those used with **open( )**. For most purposes, *mode* will be allowed to default. If you use the parameterless version of **ostrstream( )**, a dynamic array is automatically allocated.

For the single-parameter version of **istrstream( )**, *buf* is a pointer to the array that will be used as a source of characters each time input is performed on the stream. The contents of the array pointed to by *buf* must be null terminated. However, the null terminator is never read from the array.

If you wish only part of a string to be used for input, use the two-parameter form of the **istrstream** constructor. Here, only the first *size* elements of the array pointed to by *buf* will be used. This string need not be null terminated, since it is the value of *size* that determines the size of the string.

To create an array-based stream capable of input and output, use **strstream( )**. In the parameterized version, *buf* points to the string that will be used for I/O operations. The value of *size* specifies the size of the array. The value of *mode* determines how the stream operates. For normal input/output operations, *mode* will be **ios::in** | **ios::out**. For input, the array must be null terminated.

If you use the parameterless version of **strstream( )**, the buffer used for I/O will be dynamically allocated, and the mode is set for read/write operations.

Related functions are **str( )** and **open( )**.

sync_with_stdio

```
#include <iostream.h>
static void sync_with_stdio();
```

The **sync_with_stdio( )** function is a member of **ios**.

Calling **sync_with_stdio( )** allows the standard C-like I/O system to be safely used concurrently with the C++ class-based I/O system.

tellg and tellp

```
#include <iostream.h>
streampos tellg();
streampos tellp();
```

The **tellg( )** function is a member of **istream**, and **tellp( )** is a member of **ostream**.

The C++ I/O system manages two pointers associated with a file. One is the *get pointer,* which specifies where in the file the next input operation will occur. The other is the *put pointer,* which specifies where in the file the next output operation will occur. Each time an input or an output operation takes place, the appropriate pointer is automatically sequentially advanced. You can determine the current position of the get pointer by using **tellg( )** and of the put pointer by using **tellp( )**.

streampos is a type defined in IOSTREAM.H that is capable of holding the largest value that either function can return.

The values returned by **tellg( )** and **tellp( )** can be used as parameters to **seekg( )** and **seekp( )**, respectively.

Related functions are **seekg( )** and **seekp( )**.

unsetf

```
#include <iostream.h>
long unsetf(long flags);
```

The **unsetf( )** function is a member of **ios**.

The **unsetf( )** function is used to clear one or more format flags.

The flags specified by *flags* are cleared. (All other flags are unaffected.) The previous flag settings are returned.

Related functions are **setf( )** and **flags( )**.

width

```
#include <iostream.h>
int width() const;
int width(int w);
```

The **width( )** function is a member of **ios**.

To obtain the current field width, use the first form of **width( )**. This version returns the current field width.

To set the field width use the second form. Here, *w* becomes the field width, and the previous field width is returned.

Related functions are **precision( )** and **fill( )**.

write

```
#include <iostream.h>
ostream &write(const char *buf, int num);
```

The **write( )** function is a member of **ostream**.

The **write( )** function writes *num* bytes to the associated output stream from the buffer pointed to by *buf*. (Note that *buf* can also be of type **unsigned char *** or **signed char ***.) It returns a reference to the stream.

Related functions are **read( )** and **put( )**.

Chapter 13—The Standard C++ I/O System

As explained in the preceding section, there are two versions of C++'s iostream library. The old-style library was described in the preceding section. The new iostream library as defined by the ANSI/ISO standards committee is described here.

USING THE NEW IOSTREAM LIBRARY

There are two fundamental differences between the old- and new-style iostream libraries. First, the old-style library was defined in the global namespace. The new, standard iostream library is contained in the **std** namespace. Second, the old-style library uses .H header files. The new library uses the new-style headers (which don't use the .H).

To use the new, standard iostream library, include the new-style header <**iostream**> in your program. After doing that, you will usually want to bring the library into your current namespace using a statement like this:

```
using namespace std;
```

After the **using** statement, both the old and new style libraries work in much the same way. Thus, you will not need to convert much (or any) of your existing code.

It is not necessary to use the **using** statement just described. Instead, you can include an explicit namespace qualifier each time you refer to a member of the I/O classes. For example, the following explicitly refers to **cout**:

```
std::cout << "This is a test";
```

Of course, if you will be making extensive use of the iostream library, then including the **using** statement makes things less tedious.

THE BASIC I/O CLASSES

The new iostream library is defined through a rather complex hierarchy of template classes. Internally, the new iostream library does not use the same class names as the old library. For example, the lowest-level classes in the old-style library are called **streambuf** and **ios**. In the new library, they are template classes called **basic_streambuf** and **basic_ios**. Fortunately, most of the class names defined by the old iostream library have been preserved through a series of **typedef** statements which create character-based versions of the I/O classes. Here is a partial list of the mapping of template class names to their character-based versions:

Template Class	**Character-Based Class**
basic_streambuf	streambuf
basic_ios	ios
basic_istream	istream
basic_ostream	ostream
basic_iostream	iostream
basic_fstream	fstream
basic_ifstream	ifstream
basic_ofstream	ofstream

The array-based I/O classes are also supported, but deprecated. New code should use the containers described in the next section.

In addition to the character-based classes, wide-character I/O classes are also provided by the new iostream library. Their names are the same as the character-based classes except that they begin with a "w". For example, **wios** is the wide-character version of **ios**.

Since the vast majority of programmers will be using character-based I/O, those are the classes described in this book. Thus, when referring to the I/O classes, we will simply use their **typedef**ed, character-based names rather then their internal, template names. For instance, this book will use the name **ios** rather than **basic_ios**.

C++'S PREDEFINED STREAMS

When using the new iostream library the following streams are automatically opened:

Stream	**Meaning**
cin	Standard input
cout	Standard output
cerr	Standard error output
clog	Buffered version of cerr
wcin	Wide character version of cin
wcout	Wide character version of cout
wcerr	Wide character version of cerr
wclog	Wide character version of clog

By default, the standard streams are used to communicate with the console. However, in environments that support I/O redirection (such as DOS, UNIX, and Windows), the standard streams can be redirected to other devices or files.

THE streamsize TYPE

The new iostream library defines several new data types. One of the most common is called **streamsize** which is some form of integer. An object of type **streamsize** is capable of holding the largest number of bytes that will be transferred in any one I/O operation.

THE iostate TYPE

The current status of an I/O stream is described by an object of type **iostate**, which is an enumeration defined by **ios** that includes these members:

Name	Meaning
goodbit	No errors have occurred
eofbit	End-of-file is encountered
failbit	A nonfatal I/O error has occurred
badbit	A fatal I/O error has occurred

THE FORMAT FLAGS AND THE fmtflags TYPE

Each stream has associated with it a set of format flags that control the way information is formatted by a stream. The new iostream library declares an enumeration called **fmtflags** in which the following values are defined:

adjustfield	floatfield	right	skipws
basefield	hex	scientific	unitbuf
boolalpha	internal	showbase	uppercase
dec	left	showpoint	
fixed	oct	showpos	

These values are used to set or clear the format flags. These values are defined within **ios**. (Technically, the enumeration **fmtflags** is defined within **ios_base**, which is a base class for **basic_ios**, but this distinction is not important for most programming situations.)

When the **skipws** flag is set, leading whitespace characters (spaces, tabs, and newlines) are discarded when performing input on a stream. When **skipws** is cleared, whitespace characters are not discarded.

When the **left** flag is set, output is left justified. When **right** is set, output is right justified. When the **internal** flag is set, a numeric value is padded to fill a field by inserting spaces between any sign or base character. If none of these flags is set, output is right justified by default.

By default, numeric values are output in decimal. However, it is possible to change the number base. Setting the **oct** flag causes output to be displayed in octal. Setting the **hex** flag causes output to be displayed in hexadecimal. To return output to decimal, set the **dec** flag.

Setting **showbase** causes the base of numeric values to be shown. For example, if the conversion base is hexadecimal, the value 1F will be displayed as 0x1F.

By default, when scientific notation is displayed, the "e" is in lowercase. Also, when a hexadecimal value is displayed, the "x" is in lowercase. When **uppercase** is set, these characters are displayed in uppercase.

Setting **showpos** causes a leading plus sign to be displayed before positive values.

Setting **showpoint** causes a decimal point and trailing zeros to be displayed for all floating-point output—whether needed or not.

By setting the **scientific** flag, floating-point numeric values are displayed using scientific notation. When **fixed** is set, floating-point values are displayed using normal notation. When neither flag is set, the compiler chooses an appropriate method.

When **unitbuf** is set, the buffer is flushed after each insertion operation.

When **boolalpha** is set, Booleans can be input or output using the keywords **true** and **false**.

Since it is common to refer to the **oct**, **dec**, and **hex** fields, they can be collectively referred to as **ios::basefield**. Similarly, the **left**, **right**, and **internal** fields can be referred to as **ios::adjustfield**. Finally, the **scientific** and **fixed** fields can be referenced as **ios::floatfield**.

The I/O Manipulators

In addition to setting or clearing the format flags directly, you can alter the format parameters of a stream through the use of special functions called *manipulators,* which can be included in an I/O expression. The standard manipulators are shown in the following table. (Some of these manipulators will not be supported by the old iostream library.)

Manipulator	**Purpose**	**Input/Output**
boolalpha	Turns on **boolalpha** flag	Input/Output
dec	Turns on **dec** flag	Input/Ouput
endl	Output a newline character and flush the stream	Output
ends	Output a null	Output
fixed	Turns on **fixed** flag	Output
flush	Flush a stream	Output
hex	Turns on **hex** flag	Input/Output
internal	Turns on **internal** flag	Output
left	Turns on **left** flag	Output
noboolalpha	Turns off **boolalpha** flag	Input/Output
noshowbase	Turns off **showbase** flag	Output
noshowpoint	Turns off **showpoint** flag	Output
noshowpos	Turns off **showpos** flag	Output
noskipws	Turns off **skipws** flag	Input
nounitbuf	Turns off **unitbuf** flag	Output
nouppercase	Turns off **uppercase** flag	Output
oct	Turns on **oct** flag	Input/Output
resetiosflags (long *f*)	Turn off the flags specified in *f*	Input/output
right	Turns on **right** flag	Output
scientific	Turns on **scientific** flag	Output
setbase(int *base*)	Set the number base to *base*	Output
setfill(int *ch*)	Set the fill character to **ch**	Output
setiosflags (long *f*)	Turn on the flags specified in *f*	Input/output
setprecision (int *p*)	Set the number of digits of precision	Output
setw(int *w*)	Set the field width to *w*	Output
showbase	Turns on **showbase** flag	Output
showpoint	Turns on **showpoint** flag	Output
showpos	Turns on **showpos** flag	Output
skipws	Turns on **skipws** flag	Input
unitbuf	Turns on **unitbuf** flag	Output
uppercase	Turns on **uppercase** flag	Output
ws	Skip leading white space	Input

To access manipulators that take parameters, such as **setw( )**, you must include <**iomanip**> in your program.

Programming Tip

One of the most interesting format flags added by the new iostream library is **boolalpha**. This flag can be set either directly, or by using the new manipulators **boolalpha( )** or **noboolalpha( )**. What makes **boolalpha** so interesting is that setting it allows you to input and output Boolean values using the keywords **true** and **false**. Normally, you must enter 1 for true and 0 for false. For example, consider the following program:

```
// Demonstrate boolalpha format flag.
#include <iostream>
using namespace std;

int main()
{
  bool b;

  cout << "Before setting boolalpha flag: ";
  b = true;
  cout << b << " ";
  b = false;
  cout << b << endl;

  cout << "After setting boolalpha flag: ";
  b = true;
  cout << boolalpha << b << " ";
  b = false;
  cout << b << endl;

  cout << "Enter a Boolean value: ";
  cin >> boolalpha >> b;
  cout << "You entered " << b;

  return 0;
}
```

Here is a sample run:

```
Before setting boolalpha flag: 1 0
After setting boolalpha flag: true false
Enter a Boolean value: true
You entered true
```

As you can see, once the **boolalpha** flag has been set, Boolean values are input and output using the words **true** or **false**. As the program shows, you must set the **boolalpha** flag for **cin** and **cout** separately. Like all format flags, setting **boolalpha** for one stream does not imply that it is also set for another.

THE STANDARD IOSTREAM FUNCTIONS

The most commonly used of the new-style iostream functions are described next.

bad

```
#include <iostream>
bool bad() const;
```


The **bad( )** function is a member of **ios**.

The **bad( )** function returns true if a fatal I/O error has occurred in the associated stream; otherwise, false is returned.

A related function is **good( )**.

clear

```
#include <iostream>
void clear(iostate flags = goodbit);
```

The **clear( )** function is a member of **ios**.

The **clear( )** function clears the status flags associated with a stream. If *flags* is **goodbit** (as it is by default), then all error flags are cleared (reset to 0). Otherwise, the status flags will be set to whatever value is specified in *flags*.

A related function is **rdstate( )**.

eof

```
#include <iostream>
bool eof() const;
```

The **eof( )** function is a member of **ios**.

The **eof( )** function returns true when the end of the associated input file has been encountered; otherwise, it returns false.

Related functions are **bad( )**, **fail( )**, **good( )**, **rdstate( )**, and **clear( )**.

fail

```
#include <iostream>
bool fail() const;
```

The **fail( )** function is a member of **ios**.

The **fail( )** function returns true if an I/O error has occurred in the associated stream. Otherwise, it returns false.

Related functions are **good( )**, **eof( )**, **bad( )**, **clear( )**, and **rdstate( )**.

fill

```
#include <iostream>
char fill() const;
char fill(char ch);
```

The **fill( )** function is a member of **ios**.

By default, when a field needs to be filled, it is filled with spaces. However, you can specify the fill character using the **fill( )** function and specifying the new fill character in *ch.* The old fill character is returned.

To obtain the current fill character, use the first form of **fill( )**, which returns the current fill character.

Related functions are **precision( )** and **width( )**.

flags

```
#include <iostream>
fmtflags flags() const;
fmtflags flags(fmtflags f);
```

The **flags( )** function is a member of **ios**.

The first form of **flags( )** simply returns the current format flags settings of the associated stream.

The second form of **flags( )** sets all format flags associated with a stream as specified by *f*. When you use this version, the bit pattern found in *f* is copied into the format flags associated with the stream. This version also returns the previous settings.

Related functions are **unsetf( )** and **setf( )**.

13

flush

```
#include <iostream>
ostream &flush();
```

The **flush( )** function is a member of **ostream**.

The **flush( )** function causes the buffer connected to the associated output stream to be physically written to the device. The function returns a reference to its associated stream.

Related functions are **put( )** and **write( )**.

fstream, ifstream, and ofstream

```
#include <fstream>
fstream();
fstream(const char *filename,
        openmode mode = ios::in | ios::out);

ifstream();
ifstream(const char *filename, openmode mode=ios::in);

ofstream();
ofstream(const char *filename,
         openmode mode=ios::out | ios::trunc);
```

The **fstream( )**, **ifstream( )**, and **ofstream( )** functions are the constructors of the **fstream**, **ifstream**, and **ofstream** classes, respectively.

The versions of **fstream( )**, **ifstream( )**, and **ofstream( )** that take no parameters create a stream that is not associated with any file. This stream can then be linked to a file using **open( )**.

The versions of **fstream( )**, **ifstream( )**, and **ofstream( )** that take a filename for their first parameters are the most commonly used in application programs. Although it is entirely proper to open a file using the **open( )** function, most of the time you will not do so because these **ifstream**, **ofstream**, and **fstream** constructor functions automatically open the file when the stream is created. The constructor functions have the same parameters and defaults as the **open( )** function. (See "**open**" for details.) For instance, this is the most common way you will see a file opened:

```
ifstream mystream("myfile");
```

If for some reason the file cannot be opened, the value of the associated stream variable will be 0. Therefore, whether you use a constructor function to open the file or an explicit call to **open( )**, you will want to confirm that the file has actually been opened by testing the value of the stream.

The type **openmode** is defined by the **ios_base** class. See "**open**" for details.

Related functions are **close( )** and **open( )**.

gcount

```
#include <iostream>
streamsize gcount() const;
```

The **gcount( )** function is a member of **istream**.

The **gcount( )** function returns the number of characters read by the last input operation.

Related functions are **get( )**, **getline( )**, and **read( )**.

get


```
#include <iostream>
int get();
istream &get(char &ch):
istream &get(char *buf, streamsize num);
istream &get(char *buf, streamsize num, char delim);
istream &get(streambuf &buf);
istream &get(streambuf &buf, char delim);
```

The **get( )** function is a member of **istream**.

In general, **get( )** reads characters from an input stream. The parameterless form of **get( )** reads a single character from the associated stream and returns that value.

get(char &*ch*) reads a character from the associated stream and puts that value in *ch.* It returns a reference to the stream.

get(char ****buf*, streamsize** ***num*)** reads characters into the array pointed to by *buf* until either *num* − 1 characters have been read, a newline is found, or the end of the file has been encountered. The array pointed to by *buf* will be null terminated by **get( )**. If the newline character is encountered in the input stream it is not extracted. Instead, it remains in the stream until the next input operation. This function returns a reference to the stream.

get(char ****buf*, streamsize** ***num***, char** ***delim*)** reads characters into the array pointed to by *buf* until either *num* − 1 characters have been read, the character specified by *delim* has been found, or the end of the file has been encountered. The array pointed to by *buf* will be null terminated by **get( )**. If the delimiter character is encountered in the input stream it is not extracted. Instead, it remains in the stream until the next input operation. This function returns a reference to the stream.

get(streambuf &*buf*) reads characters from the input stream into the **streambuf** object. Characters are read until a newline is found or the end of the file is encountered. It returns a reference to the stream. If the newline character is encountered in the input stream, it is not extracted.

get(streambuf &*buf*, char ***delim*)** reads characters from the input stream into the **streambuf** object. Characters are read until the character specified by *delim* is found or the end of the file is encountered. It returns a reference to the stream. If the delimiter character is encountered in the input stream, it is not extracted.

Related functions are **put( )**, **read( )**, and **getline( )**.

getline

```
#include <iostream>
istream &getline(char *buf, streamsize num);
istream &getline(char *buf, streamsize num, char delim);
```

The **getline( )** function is a member of **istream**.

getline(char **buf*, streamsize *num*) reads characters into the array pointed to by *buf* until either *num* − 1 characters have been read, a newline character has been found, or the end of the file has been encountered. The array pointed to by *buf* will be null terminated by **getline( )**. If the newline character is encountered in the input stream it is extracted, but is not put into *buf*. This function returns a reference to the stream.

getline(char **buf*, streamsize *num*, char *delim*) reads characters into the array pointed to by *buf* until either *num* − 1 characters have been read, the character specified by *delim* has been found, or the end of the file has been encountered. The array pointed to by *buf* will be null terminated by **getline( )**. If the delimiter character is encountered in the input stream it is extracted, but is not put into *buf*. This function returns a reference to the stream.

Related functions are **get( )** and **read( )**.

good

```
#include <iostream>
bool good() const;
```

The **good( )** function is a member of **ios**.

The **good( )** function returns true if no I/O errors have occurred in the associated stream; otherwise, it returns false.

Related functions are **bad( )**, **fail( )**, **eof( )**, **clear( )**, and **rdstate( )**.

ignore

```
#include <iostream>
istream &ignore(streamsize num = 1, int delim = EOF);
```

The **ignore( )** function is a member of **istream**.

13

You can use the **ignore( )** member function to read and discard characters from the input stream. It reads and discards characters until either *num* characters have been ignored (1 by default) or the character specified by *delim* is encountered (**EOF** by default). If the delimiting character is encountered, it is removed from the input stream. The function returns a reference to the stream.

Related functions are **get( )** and **getline( )**.

open

```
#include <fstream>
void fstream::open(const char *filename,
                   openmode mode = ios::in | ios::out);
void ifstream::open(const char *filename,
                    openmode mode = ios::in);
void ofstream::open(const char *filename,
                    openmode mode = ios::out | ios::trunc);
```

The **open( )** function is a member of **fstream**, **ifstream**, and **ofstream**.

A file is associated with a stream by using the **open( )** function. Here, *filename* is the name of the file, which may include a path specifier. The value of *mode* determines how the file is opened. It must be one (or more) of these values:

ios::app

ios::ate

ios::binary

ios::in

ios::out

ios::trunc

You can combine two or more of these values by ORing them together.

Including **ios::app** causes all output to that file to be appended to the end. This value can only be used with files capable of output. Including **ios::ate** causes a seek to the end of the file to occur when the file is opened. Although **ios::ate** causes a seek to the end-of-file, I/O operations can still occur anywhere within the file.

The **ios::binary** value causes the file to be opened for binary I/O operations. By default, files are opened in text mode.

The **ios::in** value specifies that the file is capable of input. The **ios::out** value specifies that the file is capable of output. However, creating an **ifstream** stream implies input, creating an **ofstream** stream implies output, and opening a file using **fstream** implies both input and output.

The **ios::trunc** value causes the contents of a preexisting file by the same name to be destroyed and the file is truncated to zero length.

In all cases, if **open( )** fails, the stream will be null. Therefore, before using a file, you should test to make sure that the open operation succeeded.

Related functions are **close( )**, **fstream( )**, **ifstream( )**, and **ofstream( )**.

Programming Tip

In the old-style iostream library, the **fstream** constructor did not contain a default for the *mode* parameter. That is, it did not automatically open a stream for input and output operations. Thus, when using the old iostream library to open a stream for input and output, both **ios::in** and **ios::out** must be specified explicitly. Keep this in mind if backward compatibility with the old iostream library is a concern.

peek

```
#include <iostream>
int peek();
```

The **peek( )** function is a member of **istream**.

The **peek( )** function returns the next character in the stream or **EOF** if the end of the file is encountered. It does not, under any circumstances, remove the character from the stream.

A related function is **get( )**.

precision

```
#include <iostream>
streamsize precision() const;
streamsize precision(streamsize p);
```

The **precision( )** function is a member of **ios**.

By default, six digits of precision are displayed when floating-point values are output. However, using the second form of **precision( )** you can set this number to the value specified in *p*. The original value is returned.

The first version of **precision( )** returns the current value.

Related functions are **width( )** and **fill( )**.

put

```
#include <iostream>
ostream &put(char ch);
```

The **put( )** function is a member of **ostream**.

The **put( )** function writes *ch* to the associated output stream. It returns a reference to the stream.

Related functions are **write( )** and **get( )**.

putback

```
#include <iostream>
istream &putback(char ch);
```

The **putback( )** function is a member of **istream**.

The **putback( )** function returns *ch* to the associated input stream.

A related function is **peek( )**.

rdstate

```
#include <iostream>
iostate rdstate() const;
```

The **rdstate( )** function is a member of **ios**.

The **rdstate( )** function returns the status of the associated stream. The C++ I/O system maintains status information about the outcome of each I/O operation relative to each active stream. The current state of a stream is held in an object of type **iostate**, in which the following flags are defined:

Name	**Meaning**
goodbit	No errors have occurred.
eofbit	End-of-file is encountered.
failbit	A nonfatal I/O error has occurred.
badbit	A fatal I/O error has occurred.

These flags are enumerated inside **ios**.

rdstate( ) returns **goodbit** when no error has occurred; otherwise, an error bit has been set.

Related functions are **eof( )**, **good( )**, **bad( )**, **clear( )**, and **fail( )**.

read

```
#include <iostream>
istream &read(char *buf, streamsize num);
```

The **read( )** function is a member of **istream**.

The **read( )** function reads *num* bytes from the associated input stream and puts them in the buffer pointed to by *buf*. If the end of the file is reached before *num* characters have been read, **read( )** simply stops, and the buffer contains as many characters as were available. (See "**gcount**.") **read( )** returns a reference to the stream.

Related functions are **gcount( )**, **get( )**, **getline( )**, and **write( )**.

seekg and seekp

```
#include <iostream>
istream &seekg(off_type offset, ios::seekdir origin)
istream &seekg(pos_type position);

ostream &seekp(off_type offset, ios::seekdir origin);
ostream &seekp(pos_type position);
```

The **seekg( )** function is a member of **istream**, and the **seekp( )** function is a member of **ostream**.

In C++'s I/O system, you perform random access using the **seekg( )** and **seekp( )** functions. To this end, the C++ I/O system manages two pointers associated with a file. One is the *get pointer,* which specifies where in the file the next input operation will occur. The other is the *put pointer,* which specifies where in the file the next output operation will occur. Each time an input or an output operation takes place, the appropriate pointer is automatically sequentially advanced. However, using the **seekg( )** and **seekp( )** functions, it is possible to access the file in a nonsequential fashion.

The two-parameter version of **seekg( )** moves the get pointer *offset* number of bytes from the location specified by *origin*. The two-parameter version of **seekp( )** moves the put pointer *offset* number of bytes from the location specified by *origin*. The *offset* parameter is of type **off_type**, which is capable of containing the largest valid value that *offset* can have.

The *origin* parameter is of type **seekdir** and is an enumeration that has these values:

ios::beg	Seek from beginning
ios::cur	Seek from current position
ios::end	Seek from end

The single-parameter versions of **seekg( )** and **seekp( )** move the file pointers to the location specified by *position*. This value must have been previously obtained using a call to either **tellg( )** or **tellp( )**, respectively. **pos_type** is a type that is capable of containing the largest valid value that *position* can have. These functions return a reference to the associated stream.

Related functions are **tellg( )** and **tellp( )**.

13

setf

```
#include <iostream>
fmtflags setf(fmtflags flags);
fmtflags setf(fmtflags flags1, fmtflags flags2);
```

The **setf( )** function is a member of **ios**.

The **setf( )** function sets the format flags associated with a stream. See the discussion of format flags earlier in this section.

The first version of **setf( )** turns on the format flags specified by *flags.* (All other flags are unaffected.) For example, to turn on the **showpos** flag for **cout**, you can use this statement:

```
cout.setf(ios::showpos);
```

When you want to set more than one flag, you can OR together the values of the flags you want set.

It is important to understand that a call to **setf( )** is done relative to a specific stream. There is no concept of calling **setf( )** by itself. Put differently, there is no concept in C++ of global format status. Each stream maintains its own format status information individually.

The second version of **setf( )** affects only the flags that are set in *flags2.* The corresponding flags are first reset and then set according to the flags specified by *flags1.* Even if *flags1* contains other set flags, only those specified by *flags2* will be affected.

Both versions of **setf( )** return the previous settings of the format flags associated with the stream.

Related functions are **unsetf( )** and **flags( )**.

sync_with_stdio

```
#include <iostream>
static bool sync_with_stdio(bool sync = true);
```

The **sync_with_stdio( )** function is a member of **ios**.

Calling **sync_with_stdio( )** allows the standard C-like I/O system to be safely used concurrently with the C++ class-based I/O system. To turn off stdio synchronization, pass **false** to **sync_with_stdio( )**. The previous setting is returned—**true** for synchronized, **false** for no synchronization.

tellg and tellp

```
#include <iostream>
pos_type tellg();
pos_type tellp():
```

The **tellg( )** function is a member of **istream**, and **tellp( )** is a member of **ostream**.

The C++ I/O system manages two pointers associated with a file. One is the *get pointer,* which specifies where in the file the next input operation will occur. The other is the *put pointer,* which specifies where in the file the next output operation will occur. Each time an input or an output operation takes place, the appropriate pointer is automatically sequentially advanced. You can determine the current position of the get pointer using **tellg( )** and of the put pointer using **tellp( )**.

pos_type is a type that is capable of holding the largest value that either function can return.

The values returned by **tellg( )** and **tellp( )** can be used as parameters to **seekg( )** and **seekp( )**, respectively.

Related functions are **seekg( )** and **seekp( )**.

unsetf

```
#include <iostream>
void unsetf(fmtflags flags);
```

The **unsetf( )** function is a member of **ios**.

The **unsetf( )** function is used to clear one or more format flags.

The flags specified by *flags* are cleared. (All other flags are unaffected.)

Related functions are **setf( )** and **flags( )**.

width

```
#include <iostream>
streamsize width() const;
streamsize width(streamsize w);
```

The **width( )** function is a member of **ios**.

To obtain the current field width, use the first form of **width( )**. This version returns the current field width.

To set the field width use the second form. Here, *w* becomes the field width, and the previous field width is returned.

Related functions are **precision( )** and **fill( )**.

write

```
#include <iostream>
ostream &write(const char *buf, streamsize num);
```

The **write( )** function is a member of **ostream**.

The **write( )** function writes *num* bytes to the associated output stream from the buffer pointed to by *buf.* It returns a reference to the stream.

Related functions are **read( )** and **put( )**.

Chapter 14—The C++ Standard Template Library

One of the major efforts that took place during the C++ standardization process was the inclusion of the *standard template library,* or *STL.* The STL provides general purpose, templatized classes and functions that implement many popular and commonly used algorithms and data structures. For example, it includes support for vectors, lists, queues, and stacks. It also defines various routines that access them. Because the STL is constructed from template classes, the algorithms and data structures can be applied to nearly any type of data.

The STL is a large library and not all of its features can be fully described in this book. Also, the version of the STL described here is the one specified by ANSI/ISO C++ standardization committee. Your compiler may present a slightly different version of the STL, so be sure to check its documentation.

AN OVERVIEW OF CONTAINERS, ALGORITHMS, AND ITERATORS

The STL consists of three items: *containers, algorithms,* and *iterators.* These items work in conjunction with one another to provide off-the-shelf solutions to a variety of programming problems. Each is briefly described here.

14

Containers

Containers are objects that hold other objects. There are several different types of containers. For example, the **vector** class defines a dynamic array, **queue** creates a queue, and **list** provides a linear list. In addition to the basic containers, the STL also defines *associative containers,* which allow efficient retrieval of values based on keys. For example, a **map** provides access to values with unique keys. Thus, a **map** stores a key/value pair and allows a value to be retrieved given its key.

Each container class defines a set of functions that can be applied to the container. For example, a list container includes functions that insert, delete, and merge elements.

Algorithms

Algorithms act on containers. They include capabilities for initializing, sorting, searching, and transforming the contents of containers. Many algorithms operate on a *sequence,* which is a linear list of elements within a container.

Iterators

Iterators are objects that are, more or less, pointers. They give you the ability to access the contents of a container in much the same way that you would use a pointer to access an array. There are five types of iterators:

Iterator	Access Allowed
Random Access	Store and retrieve values; elements can be accessed randomly
Bidirectional	Store and retrieve values; forward- and backward-moving
Forward	Store and retrieve values; forward-moving only
Input	Retrieve, but not store values; forward-moving only
Output	Store, but not retrieve values; forward-moving only

In general, an iterator that has greater access capabilities can be used in place of one that has lesser capabilities. For example, a forward iterator can be used in place of an input iterator.

Iterators are handled the same as pointers. You can increment and decrement them. You can apply the * operator to them.

Iterators are declared using the **iterator** type defined by the various containers.

When referring to the various iterator types generically, this book uses the following terms:

Term	**Represents**
BiIter	Bidirectional iterator
ForIter	Forward iterator
InIter	Input iterator
OutIter	Output iterator
RandIter	Random access iterator

The STL also supports *reverse iterators.* Reverse iterators are either bidirectional or random access iterators that move through a sequence in the reverse direction. Thus, if a reverse iterator points to the end of a sequence, incrementing that iterator will cause it to point one element before the end.

ALLOCATORS

Each container has defined for it an *allocator,* which is an object of class **allocator**. Allocators manage the allocation of memory when a new container is created.

PREDICATES AND COMPARISON FUNCTIONS

Several of the algorithms and containers use a special type of function called a *predicate.* There are two variations of predicates: unary and binary. A unary predicate takes one argument. A binary predicate takes two arguments. These functions return true/false results. But the precise conditions that make them return true or false are defined by you. In the descriptions that follow, when a unary predicate function is required, it will be notated using the type **UnPred**. When a binary predicate is required, the type **BinPred** will be used. In a binary predicate, the arguments are always in the order of *first,second* relative to the function that calls the predicate. For both unary and binary predicates, the arguments will contain values of the type of objects being stored by the container.

Some algorithms and classes use a special type of binary predicate that compares two elements. Comparison functions return true if their first argument is less than their second. Comparison functions will be notated using the type **Comp**.

THE UTILITY AND FUNCTIONAL HEADERS

In addition to the headers required by the various STL classes, the C++ standard library includes the <**utility**> and <**functional**> headers, which provide support for the STL. For example, in <**utility**> is defined the template class **pair**, which can hold a pair of values. The template function **less( )**, declared within <**functional**>, determines when one object is less than another.

The templates in <**functional**> allow you to construct objects that define **operator( )**. These are called *function objects,* and they can be used in place of function pointers in many places. It is beyond the scope of this quick reference to describe these headers.

Programming Tip

Containers, algorithms, and iterators work together. The best way to understand how is to see an example. The following program demonstrates the **vector** container. A **vector** is similar to an array. However, it has the advantage that it automatically handles its own storage requirements, growing if necessary. A **vector** provides methods so that you can determine its size and add or remove elements.

The following program illustrates the use of a **vector** class:

```
// A short example that demonstrates vector.
#include <iostream>
#include <vector>
using namespace std;

int main()
{
  vector<int> v; // create zero-length vector
  int i;

  // display original size of v
  cout << "size = " << v.size() << endl;

  /* put values onto end of vector --
     vector will grow as needed. */
  for(i=0; i<10; i++) v.push_back(i);
```

```
  // display current size of v
  cout << "size now = " << v.size() << endl;

  // can access vector contents using subscripting
  for(i=0; i<10; i++) cout << v[i] << " ";
  cout << endl;

  // can access vector's first and last element
  cout << "front = " << v.front() << endl;
  cout << "back = " << v.back() << endl;

  // access via iterator
  vector<int>::iterator p = v.begin();
  while(p != v.end()) {
    cout << *p << " ";
    p++;
  }

  return 0;
}
```

The output from this program is

```
size = 0
size now = 10
0 1 2 3 4 5 6 7 8 9
front = 0
back = 9
0 1 2 3 4 5 6 7 8 9
```

In this program, the vector is initially created with zero length. The **push_back( )** member function puts values onto the end of the vector, expanding its size as needed. The **size( )** function displays the size of the vector. The vector can be indexed like a normal array. It can also be accessed using an iterator. The function **begin( )** returns an iterator to the start of the vector. The function **end( )** returns an iterator to the end of the vector.

One other point: Notice how the iterator **p** was declared. The type **iterator** is defined by several of the container classes.

THE CONTAINER CLASSES

The containers defined by the STL are shown here:

Container	Description	Required Header
bitset	A set of bits	<bitset>
deque	A double-ended queue	<deque>
list	A linear list	<list>
map	Stores key/value pairs in which each key is associated with only one value	<map>
multimap	Stores key/value pairs in which one key can be associated with two or more values	<map>
multiset	A set in which each element is not necessarily unique	<set>
priority_queue	A priority queue	<queue>
queue	A queue	<queue>
set	A set in which each element is unique	<set>
stack	A stack	<stack>
vector	A dynamic array	<vector>

The **string** class, which manages character strings, is also a container, but it is discussed in Chapter 15.

Each of the containers is summarized in the following sections. Since the containers are implemented using template classes, various placeholder data types are used. In the descriptions, the generic type **T** represents the type of data stored by a container, and **Size** represents some integral type.

Since the names of the placeholder types in a template class are arbitrary, the container classes declare **typedef**ed versions of these types. This makes the type names concrete. Some of the most common **typedef** names are shown here:

size_type	Some integral type equivalent to **size_t**
reference	A reference to an element
const_reference	A **const** reference to an element
iterator	An iterator
const_iterator	A **const** iterator
reverse_iterator	A reverse iterator
const_reverse_iterator	A **const** reverse iterator
value_type	The type of a value stored in a container
allocator_type	The type of the allocator
key_type	The type of a key
key_compare	The type of a function that compares two keys
value_compare	The type of a function that compares two values

bitset

The **bitset** class supports operations on a set of bits. Its template specification is

template <size_t *N*> class bitset;

Here, *N* specifies the length of the bitset, in bits. It has the following constructors:

bitset( );
bitset(unsigned long *bits*);
explicit bitset(const string &*s*, size_t *i* = 0, size_t *num* = −1);

The first form constructs an empty bitset. The second form constructs a bitset that has its bits set according to those specified in *bits.* The third form constructs a bitset using the string *s*, beginning at *i*. The string must contain only 1's and 0's. Only *num* or *s*.**size( )** −*i* values are used, whichever is less.

The output operators << and >> are defined for **bitset**.

bitset contains the following member functions:

Member	Description
bool any( ) const;	Returns true if any bit in the invoking bitset is 1; returns false otherwise
size_type count( ) const;	Returns the number of 1 bits
bitset<N> &flip( );	Reverses the state of all bits in the invoking bitset and returns ***this**
bitset<N> &flip(size_t *i*);	Reverses the bit in position *i* in the invoking bitset and returns ***this**
bool none( ) const;	Returns true if no bits are set in the invoking bitset
bool operator !=(const bitset<N> &*op2*) const;	Returns true if the invoking bitset differs from the one specified by right-hand operator, *op2*
bool operator ==(const bitset<N> &*op2*) const;	Returns true if the invoking bitset is the same as the one specified by right-hand operator, *op2*
bitset<N> &operator &=(const bitset<N> &*op2*);	ANDs each bit in the invoking bitset with the corresponding bit in *op2* and leaves the result in the invoking bitset; returns ***this**
bitset<N> &operator ^ =(const bitset<N> &*op2*);	XORs each bit in the invoking bitset with the corresponding bit in *op2* and leaves the result in the invoking bitset; returns ***this**
bitset<N> &operator |=(const bitset<N> &*op2*);	ORs each bit in the invoking bitset with the corresponding bit in *op2* and leaves the result in the invoking bitset; returns ***this**

Member	Description
bitset<N> &operator~( ) const;	Reverses the state of all bits in the invoking bitset and returns ***this**
bitset<N> &operator <<=(size_t *num*);	Left shifts each bit in the invoking bitset *num* positions and leaves the result in the invoking bitset; returns ***this**
bitset<N> &operator >>=(size_t *num*);	Right shifts each bit in the invoking bitset *num* positions and leaves the result in the invoking bitset; returns ***this**
reference operator [ ](size_type *i*);	Returns a reference to bit *i* in the invoking bitset
bitset<N> &reset( );	Clears all bits in the invoking bitset and returns ***this**
bitset<N> &reset(size_t *i*);	Clears the bit in position *i* in the invoking bitset and returns ***this**
bitset<N> &set( );	Sets all bits in the invoking bitset and returns ***this**
bitset<N> &set(size_t *i*, int *val* = 1);	Sets the bit in position *i* to the value specified by *val* in the invoking bitset and returns ***this**. Any nonzero value for *val* is assumed to be 1.
size_t size( ) const;	Returns the number of bits that the bitset can hold
bool test(size_t *i*);	Returns the state of the bit in position *i*
string to_string( ) const;	Returns a string that contains a representation of the bit pattern in the invoking bitset
unsigned long to_ulong( ) const;	Converts the invoking bitset into an unsigned long integer

deque

The **deque** class supports a double-ended queue. Its template specification is

```
template <class T, class Allocator = allocator<T>>
  class deque
```

Here, **T** is the type of data stored in the **deque**. It has the following constructors:

```
explicit deque(const Allocator &a = Allocator( ) );
explicit deque(size_type num, const T &val = T ( ),
               const Allocator &a = Allocator( ));
deque(const deque<T, Allocator> &ob);
template <class InIter> deque(InIter start, InIter end,
                        const Allocator &a = Allocator( ));
```

The first form constructs an empty deque. The second form constructs a deque that has *num* elements with the value *val*. The third form constructs a deque that contains the same elements as *ob*. The fourth form constructs a queue that contains the elements in the range specified by *start* and *end*.

The following comparison operators are defined for **deque**: ==, <, <=, !=, >, and >=.

deque contains the following member functions:

Member	**Description**
template <class InIter> void assign(InIter *start*, InIter *end*);	Assigns the deque the sequence defined by *start* and *end*
template <class Size, class T> void assign(Size *num*, const T &*val* = T( ));	Assigns the deque *num* elements of value *val*
reference at(size_type *i*); const_reference at(size_type *i*) const;	Returns a reference to the element specified by *i*
reference back( ); const_reference back( ) const;	Returns a reference to the last element in the deque
iterator begin( ); const_iterator begin( ) const;	Returns an iterator to the first element in the deque
void clear( );	Removes all elements from the deque
bool empty( ) const;	Returns true if the invoking deque is empty and false otherwise
const_iterator end( ) const; iterator end( );	Returns an iterator to the end of the deque

14

Member	Description
iterator erase(iterator *i*);	Removes the element pointed to by *i;* returns an iterator to the element after the one removed
iterator erase(iterator *start*, iterator *end*);	Removes the elements in the range *start* to *end;* returns an iterator to the element after the last element removed
reference front( ); const_reference front( ) const;	Returns a reference to the first element in the deque
allocator_type get_allocator( ) const;	Returns deque's allocator
iterator insert(iterator *i*, const T &*val* = T( ));	Inserts *val* immediately before the element specified by *i*. An iterator to the element is returned.
void insert(iterator *i*, size_type *num*, const T & *val*);	Inserts *num* copies of *val* immediately before the element specified by *i*
template <class InIter> void insert(iterator *i*, InIter *start*, InIter *end*);	Inserts the sequence defined by *start* and *end* immediately before the element specified by *i*
size_type max_size( ) const;	Returns the maximum number of elements that the deque can hold
reference operator[ ](size_type *i*) const; const_reference operator[ ](size_type *i*) const;	Returns a reference to the *i*th element
void pop_back( );	Removes the last element in the deque
void pop_front( );	Removes the first element in the deque
void push_back(const T &*val*);	Adds an element with the value specified by *val* to the end of the deque
void push_front(const T &*val*);	Adds an element with the value specified by *val* to the front of the deque
reverse_iterator rbegin( ); const_reverse_iterator rbegin( ) const;	Returns a reverse iterator to the end of the deque
reverse_iterator rend( ); const_reverse_iterator rend( ) const;	Returns a reverse iterator to the start of the deque

Member	Description
void resize(size_type *num*, T *val* = T ( ));	Changes the size of the deque to that specified by *num*. If the deque must be lengthened, then elements with the value specified by *val* are added to the end.
size_type size( ) const;	Returns the number of elements currently in the deque
void swap(deque<T, Allocator> &*ob*);	Exchanges the elements stored in the invoking deque with those in *ob*

list

The **list** class supports a list. Its template specification is

template <class T, class Allocator = allocator<T>> class list

Here, **T** is the type of data stored in the list. It has the following constructors:

explicit list(const Allocator &*a* = Allocator( ));

explicit list(size_type *num*, const T &*val* = T ( ),
const Allocator &*a* = Allocator( ));

list(const list<T, Allocator> &*ob*);

template <class InIter>list(InIter *start*, InIter *end*,
const Allocator &*a* = Allocator( ));

The first form constructs an empty list. The second form constructs a list that has *num* elements with the value *val*. The third form constructs a list that contains the same elements as *ob*. The fourth form constructs a list that contains the elements in the range specified by *start* and *end*.

The following comparison operators are defined for **list**: ==, <, <=, !=, >, and >=.

list contains the following member functions:

Member	**Description**
template <class InIter> void assign(InIter *start*, InIter *end*);	Assigns the list the sequence defined by *start* and *end*
template <class Size, class T> void assign(Size *num*, const T &*val* = T( ));	Assigns the list *num* elements of value *val*
reference back( ); const_reference back( ) const;	Returns a reference to the last element in the list
iterator begin( ); const_iterator begin( ) const;	Returns an iterator to the first element in the list
void clear( );	Removes all elements from the list
bool empty( ) const;	Returns true if the invoking list is empty and false otherwise
iterator end( ); const_iterator end( ) const;	Returns an iterator to the end of the list
iterator erase(iterator *i*);	Removes the element pointed to by *i*; returns an iterator to the element after the one removed
iterator erase(iterator *start*, iterator *end*);	Removes the elements in the range *start* to *end*; returns an iterator to the element after the last element removed
reference front( ); const_reference front( ) const;	Returns a reference to the first element in the list
allocator_type get_allocator( ) const;	Returns list's allocator
iterator insert(iterator *i*, const T &*val* = T( ));	Inserts *val* immediately before the element specified by *i*. An iterator to the element is returned.
void insert(iterator *i*, size_type *num*, const T & *val*);	Inserts *num* copies of *val* immediately before the element specified by *i*
template <class InIter> void insert(iterator *i*, InIter *start*, InIter *end*);	Inserts the sequence defined by *start* and *end* immediately before the element specified by *i*
size_type max_size( ) const;	Returns the maximum number of elements that the list can hold

Member	Description
void merge(list<T, Allocator> &*ob*); template <class Comp> void merge(list<T, Allocator> &*ob*, Comp *cmpfn*);	Merges the ordered list contained in *ob* with the ordered invoking list. The result is ordered. After the merge, the list contained in *ob* is empty. In the second form, a comparison function can be specified that determines when one element is less than another.
void pop_back( );	Removes the last element in the list
void pop_front( );	Removes the first element in the list
void push_back(const T &*val*);	Adds an element with the value specified by *val* to the end of the list
void push_front(const T &*val*);	Adds an element with the value specified by *val* to the front of the list
reverse_iterator rbegin( ); const_reverse_iterator rbegin( ) const;	Returns a reverse iterator to the end of the list
void remove(const T &*val*);	Removes elements with the value *val* from the list
template <class UnPred> void remove_if(UnPred *pr*);	Removes elements for which the unary predicate *pr* is true
reverse_iterator rend( ); const_reverse_iterator rend( ) const;	Returns a reverse iterator to the start of the list
void resize(size_type *num*, T *val* = T ( ));	Changes the size of the list to that specified by *num*. If the list must be lengthened, those elements with the value specified by *val* are added to the end.
void reverse( );	Reverses the invoking list
size_type size( ) const;	Returns the number of elements currently in the list

void sort( );
template <class Comp>
void sort(Comp *cmpfn*);
	Sorts the list. The second form sorts the list using the comparison function *fn* to determine when one element is less than another.

14

Member	Description
void splice(iterator *i*, list<T, Allocator> &*ob*);	The contents of *ob* are inserted into the invoking list at the location pointed to by *i*. After the operation, *ob* is empty.
void splice(iterator *i*, list<T, Allocator> &*ob*, iterator *el*);	The element pointed to by *el* is removed from the list *ob* and stored in the invoking list at the location pointed to by *i*.
void splice(iterator *i*, list<T, Allocator> &*ob*, iterator *start*, iterator *end*);	The range defined by *start* and *end* is removed from *ob* and stored in the invoking list beginning at the location pointed to by *i*
void swap(list<T, Allocator> &*ob*);	Exchanges the elements stored in the invoking list with those in *ob*
void unique( ); template <class BinPred> void unique(BinPred *pr*);	Removes duplicate elements from the invoking list. The second form uses *pr* to determine uniqueness.

map

The **map** class supports an associative container in which unique keys are mapped with values. Its template specification is shown here:

```
template <class Key, class T, class Comp = less<Key>,
   class Allocator = allocator<T>> class map
```

Here, **Key** is the data type of the keys, **T** is the data type of the values being stored (mapped), and **Comp** is a function that compares two keys. It has the following constructors:

```
explicit map(const Comp &cmpfn = Comp( ),
             const Allocator &a = Allocator( ) );

map(const map<Key, T, Comp, Allocator> &ob);

template <class InIter> map(InIter start, InIter end,
                            const Comp &cmpfn = Comp( ),
                            const Allocator &a = Allocator( ));
```

The first form constructs an empty map. The second form constructs a map that contains the same elements as *ob*. The third form constructs a map that contains the elements in the range specified by *start* and *end*. The function specified by *cmpfn*, if present, determines the ordering of the map.

The following comparison operators are defined for **map**: ==, <, <=, !=, >, and >=.

The member functions contained by **map** are shown here. In the descriptions, **key_type** is the type of the key, and **value_type** represents **pair<Key, T>**.

Member	Description
iterator begin( ); const_iterator begin( ) const;	Returns an iterator to the first element in the map
void clear( );	Removes all elements from the map
size_type count(const key_type &*k*) const;	Returns the number of times *k* occurs in the map (1 or 0)
bool empty( ) const;	Returns true if the invoking map is empty and false otherwise
iterator end( ); const_iterator end( ) const;	Returns an iterator to the end of the map

pair<iterator, iterator>
equal_range(const key_type &*k*);
pair<const_iterator, const_iterator>
equal_range(const key_type &*k*) const;
	Returns a pair of iterators that point to the first and last elements in the map that contain the specified key

void erase(iterator *i*);	Removes the element pointed to by *i*
void erase(iterator *start*, iterator *end*);	Removes the elements in the range *start* to *end*
size_type erase(const key_type &*k*);	Removes from the map elements that have keys with the value *k*

Member	**Description**
iterator find(const key_type &*k*); const_iterator find(const key_type &*k*) const;	Returns an iterator to the specified key. If the key is not found, then an iterator to the end of the map is returned.
allocator_type get_allocator( ) const;	Returns map's allocator
iterator insert(iterator *i*, const value_type &*val*);	Inserts *val* at or after the element specified by *i*. An iterator to the element is returned.
template <class InIter> void insert(InIter *start*, InIter *end*);	Inserts a range of elements
pair<iterator, bool> insert(const value_type &*val*);	Inserts *val* into the invoking map. An iterator to the element is returned. The element is only inserted if it does not already exist. If the element was inserted, pair<iterator, true> is returned. Otherwise, pair<iterator, false> is returned.
key_compare key_comp( ) const;	Returns the function object that compares keys
iterator lower_bound(const key_type &*k*); const_iterator lower_bound(const key_type &*k*) const;	Returns an iterator to the first element in the map with the key equal to or greater than *k*
size_type max_size( ) const;	Returns the maximum number of elements that the map can hold
reference operator[ ](const key_type &*i*);	Returns a reference to the element specified by *i*. If this element does not exist, it is inserted.
reverse_iterator rbegin( ); const_reverse_iterator rbegin( ) const;	Returns a reverse iterator to the end of the map
reverse_iterator rend( ); const_reverse_iterator rend( ) const;	Returns a reverse iterator to the start of the map

Member	Description
size_type size( ) const;	Returns the number of elements currently in the map
void swap(map<Key, T, Comp, Allocator> &*ob*);	Exchanges the elements stored in the invoking map with those in *ob*
iterator upper_bound(const key_type &*k*); const_iterator upper_bound(const key_type &*k*) const;	Returns an iterator to the first element in the map with the key greater than *k*
value_compare value_comp( ) const;	Returns the function object that compares values

multimap

The **multimap** class supports an associative container in which possibly nonunique keys are mapped with values. Its template specification is shown here:

```
template <class Key, class T, class Comp = less<Key>,
   class Allocator = allocator<T>> class multimap
```

Here, **Key** is the data type of the keys, **T** is the data type of the values being stored (mapped), and **Comp** is a function that compares two keys. It has the following constructors:

```
explicit multimap(const Comp &cmpfn = Comp( ),
                  const Allocator &a = Allocator( ) );

multimap(const multimap<Key, T, Comp, Allocator> &ob);

template <class InIter> multimap(InIter start, InIter end,
                        const Comp &cmpfn = Comp( ),
                        const Allocator &a = Allocator( ) );
```


The first form constructs an empty multimap. The second form constructs a multimap that contains the same elements as *ob*. The third form constructs a multimap that contains the elements in the range specified by *start* and *end*. The function specified by *cmpfn*, if present, determines the ordering of the multimap.

The following comparison operators are defined by **multimap**: ==, <, <=, !=, >, and >=.

The member functions contained by **multimap** are shown here. In the descriptions, **key_type** is the type of the key, **T** is the value, and **value_type** represents **pair<Key, T>**.

Member	**Description**
iterator begin( ); const_iterator begin( ) const;	Returns an iterator to the first element in the multimap
void clear( );	Removes all elements from the multimap
size_type count(const key_type &*k*) const;	Returns the number of times *k* occurs in the multimap
bool empty( ) const;	Returns true if the invoking multimap is empty and false otherwise
iterator end( ); const_iterator end( ) const;	Returns an iterator to the end of the multimap

pair<iterator, iterator>
equal_range(const key_type &*k*);
pair<const_iterator, const_iterator>
equal_range(const key_type &*k*) const;
	Returns a pair of iterators that point to the first and last elements in the multimap that contain the specified key

void erase(iterator *i*);	Removes the element pointed to by *i*
void erase(iterator *start*, iterator *end*);	Removes the elements in the range *start* to *end*
size_type erase(const key_type &*k*);	Removes from the multimap elements that have keys with the value *k*
iterator find(const key_type &*k*); const_iterator find(const key_type &*k*) const;	Returns an iterator to the specified key. If the key is not found, then an iterator to the end of the multimap is returned.
allocator_type get_allocator( ) const;	Returns multimap's allocator

Member	Description
iterator insert(iterator *i*, const value_type &*val*);	Inserts *val* at or after the element specified by *i*. An iterator to the element is returned.
template <class InIter> void insert(InIter *start*, InIter *end*);	Inserts a range of elements
iterator insert(const value_type &*val*);	Inserts *val* into the invoking multimap
key_compare key_comp( ) const;	Returns the function object that compares keys
iterator lower_bound(const key_type &*k*); const_iterator lower_bound(const key_type &*k*) const;	Returns an iterator to the first element in the multimap with the key equal to or greater than *k*
size_type max_size( ) const;	Returns the maximum number of elements that the multimap can hold
reverse_iterator rbegin( ); const_reverse_iterator rbegin( ) const;	Returns a reverse iterator to the end of the multimap
reverse_iterator rend( ); const_reverse_iterator rend( ) const;	Returns a reverse iterator to the start of the multimap
size_type size( ) const;	Returns the number of elements currently in the multimap
void swap(multimap<Key, T, Comp, Allocator> &*ob*);	Exchanges the elements stored in the invoking multimap with those in *ob*
iterator upper_bound(const key_type&*k*); const_iterator upper_bound(const key_type &*k*) const;	Returns an iterator to the first element in the multimap with the key greater than *k*
value_compare value_comp( ) const;	Returns the function object that compares values

multiset

The **multiset** class supports a set in which possibly non-unique keys are mapped with values. Its template specification is shown here:

template <class Key, class Comp = less<Key>,
class Allocator = allocator<Key>> class multiset

Here, **Key** is the data type of the keys, and **Comp** is a function that compares two keys. It has the following constructors:

explicit multiset(const Comp &*cmpfn* = Comp( ),
const Allocator &*a* = Allocator( ));

multiset(const multiset<Key, Comp, Allocator> &*ob*);

template <class InIter> multiset(InIter *start*, InIter *end*,
const Comp &*cmpfn* = Comp( ),
const Allocator &*a* = Allocator( ));

The first form constructs an empty multiset. The second form constructs a multiset that contains the same elements as *ob*. The third form constructs a multiset that contains the elements in the range specified by *start* and *end*. The function specified by *cmpfn*, if present, determines the ordering of the set.

The following comparison operators are defined for **multiset**: ==, <, <=, !=, >, and >=.

The member functions contained by **multiset** are shown here. In the descriptions, both **key_type** and **value_type** are **typedef**s for **Key**.

Member	**Description**
iterator begin( ); const_iterator begin( ) const;	Returns an iterator to the first element in the multiset
void clear( );	Removes all elements from the multiset

Member	Description
size_type count(const key_type &*k*) const;	Returns the number of times *k* occurs in the multiset
bool empty( ) const;	Returns true if the invoking multiset is empty and false otherwise
iterator end( ); const_iterator end( ) const;	Returns an iterator to the end of the multiset
pair<iterator, iterator> equal_range(const key_type &*k*) const;	Returns a pair of iterators that point to the first and last elements in the multiset that contain the specified key
void erase(iterator *i*);	Removes the element pointed to by *i*
void erase(iterator *start*, iterator *end*);	Removes the elements in the range *start* to *end*
size_type erase(const key_type &*k*);	Removes from the multiset elements that have keys with the value *k*
iterator find(const key_type &*k*) const;	Returns an iterator to the specified key. If the key is not found, then an iterator to the end of the multiset is returned.
allocator_type get_allocator( ) const;	Returns multiset's allocator
iterator insert(iterator *i*, const value_type &*val*);	Inserts *val* at or after the element specified by *i*. An iterator to the element is returned.
template <class InIter> void insert(InIter *start*, InIter *end*);	Inserts a range of elements
iterator insert(const value_type &*val*);	Inserts *val* into the invoking multiset. An iterator to the element is returned
key_compare key_comp( ) const;	Returns the function object that compares keys
iterator lower_bound(const key_type &*k*) const;	Returns an iterator to the first element in the multiset with the key equal to or greater than *k*

Member	Description
size_type max_size( ) const;	Returns the maximum number of elements that the multiset can hold
reverse_iterator rbegin( ); const_reverse_iterator rbegin( ) const;	Returns a reverse iterator to the end of the multiset
reverse_iterator rend( ); const_reverse_iterator rend( ) const;	Returns a reverse iterator to the start of the multiset
size_type size( ) const;	Returns the number of elements currently in the multiset
void swap(multiset<Key, Comp, Allocator> &*ob*);	Exchanges the elements stored in the invoking multiset with those in *ob*
iterator upper_bound(const key_type &*k*) const;	Returns an iterator to the first element in the multiset with the key greater than *k*
value_compare value_comp( ) const;	Returns the function object that compares values

queue

The **queue** class supports a single-ended queue. Its template specification is shown here:

template <class T, class Container = deque<T>> class queue

Here, **T** is the type of data being stored, and **Container** is the type of container used to hold the queue. It has the following constructor:

explicit queue(const Container &*cnt* = Container( ));

The **queue( )** constructor creates an empty queue. By default it uses a **deque** as a container, but a **queue** can only be accessed in a first-in, first-out manner. You can also use a **list** as a container for a queue. The container is held in a protected object called **c** of type **Container**.

The following comparison operators are defined for **queue**: ==, <, <=, !=, >, and >=.

queue contains the following member functions:

Member	Description
value_type &back( ); const value_type &back( ) const;	Returns a reference to the last element in the queue
bool empty( ) const;	Returns true if the invoking queue is empty and false otherwise
value_type &front( ); const value_type &front( ) const;	Returns a reference to the first element in the queue
void pop( );	Removes the first element in the queue
void push(const T &*val*);	Adds an element with the value specified by *val* to the end of the queue
size_type size( ) const;	Returns the number of elements currently in the queue

priority_queue

The **priority_queue** class supports a single-ended priority queue. Its template specification is shown here:

```
template <class T, class Container = vector<T>,
  class Comp = less<Container::value_type>>
  class priority_queue
```

Here, **T** is the type of data being stored. **Container** is the type of container used to hold the queue, and **Comp** specifies the comparison function that determines when one member for the priority queue is lower in priority than another. It has the following constructors:

```
explicit priority_queue(const Comp &cmpfn = Comp( ),
                        Container &cnt = Container( ) );

template <class InIter> priority_queue(InIter start, InIter end,
                        const Comp &cmpfn = Comp( ),
                        Container &cnt = Container( ) );
```

The first **priority_queue( )** constructor creates an empty priority queue. The second creates a priority queue that contains the elements specified by the range *start* and *end*. By default it uses a **vector** as a container. You can also use a **deque** as a container for a queue. The container is held in a protected object called **c** of type **Container**.

priority_queue contains the following member functions:

Member	**Description**
bool empty( ) const;	Returns true if the invoking priority queue is empty and false otherwise
void pop( );	Removes the first element in the priority queue
void push(const T &*val*);	Adds an element to the priority queue
size_type size( ) const;	Returns the number of elements currently in the priority queue
value_type &top( ); cont value_type &top( ) const;	Returns a reference to the element with the highest priority. The element is not removed.

set

The **set** class supports a set in which possibly unique keys are mapped with values. Its template specification is shown here:

```
template <class Key, class Comp = less<Key>,
  class Allocator = allocator<Key>> class set
```

Here, **Key** is the data type of the keys and **Comp** is a function that compares two keys. It has the following constructors:

```
explicit set(const Comp &cmpfn = Comp( ),
             const Allocator &a = Allocator( ));

set(const set<Key, Comp, Allocator> &ob);

template <class InIter> set(InIter start, InIter end,
                            const Comp &cmpfn = Comp( ),
                            const Allocator &a = Allocator( ));
```

The first form constructs an empty set. The second form constructs a set that contains the same elements as *ob*. The third form constructs a set that contains the elements in the range specified by *start* and *end*. The function specified by *cmpfn,* if present, determines the ordering of the set.

The following comparison operators are defined for **set**: ==, <, <=, !=, >, and >=.

The member functions contained by **set** are shown here. In the descriptions, both **key_type** and **value_type** are **typedefs** for **Key**.

Member	**Description**
iterator begin( ); const_iterator begin( ) const;	Returns an iterator to the first element in the set
void clear( );	Removes all elements from the set
size_type count(const key_type &*k*) const;	Returns the number of times *k* occurs in the set
bool empty( ) const;	Returns true if the invoking set is empty and false otherwise
const_iterator end( ) const; iterator end( );	Returns an iterator to the end of the list

Member	**Description**
pair<iterator, iterator> equal_range(const key_type &*k*) const;	Returns a pair of iterators that point to the first and last elements in the set that contain the specified key
void erase(iterator *i*);	Removes the element pointed to by *i*
void erase(iterator *start*, iterator *end*);	Removes the elements in the range *start* to *end*
size_type erase(const key_type &*k*);	Removes from the set elements that have keys with the value *k*. The number of elements removed is returned.
iterator find(const key_type &*k*) const;	Returns an iterator to the specified key. If the key is not found, then an iterator to the end of the set is returned.
allocator_type get_allocator( ) const;	Returns set's allocator
iterator insert(iterator *i*, const value_type &*val*);	Inserts *val* at or after the element specified by *i*. Duplicate elements are not inserted. An iterator to the element is returned.
template <class InIter> void insert(InIter *start*, InIter *end*);	Inserts a range of elements. Duplicate elements are not inserted.
pair<iterator, bool> insert(const value_type &*val*);	Inserts *val* into the invoking set. An iterator to the element is returned. The element is inserted only if it does not already exist. If the element was inserted, pair<iterator, true> is returned. Otherwise, pair<iterator, false> is returned.
iterator lower_bound(const key_type &*k*) const;	Returns an iterator to the first element in the set with the key equal to or greater than *k*
key_compare key_comp( ) const;	Returns the function object that compares keys

Member	Description
size_type max_size( ) const;	Returns the maximum number of elements that the set can hold
reverse_iterator rbegin( ); const_reverse_iterator rbegin( ) const;	Returns a reverse iterator to the end of the set
reverse_iterator rend( ); const_reverse_iterator rend( ) const;	Returns a reverse iterator to the start of the set
size_type size( ) const;	Returns the number of elements currently in the set
void swap(set<Key, Comp, Allocator> &*ob*);	Exchanges the elements stored in the invoking set with those in *ob*
iterator upper_bound(const key_type &*k*) const;	Returns an iterator to the first element in the set with the key greater than *k*
value_compare value_comp( ) const;	Returns the function object that compares values

stack

The **stack** class supports a stack. Its template specification is shown here:

```
template <class T, class Container = deque<T>> class stack
```

Here, **T** is the type of data being stored, and **Container** is the type of container used to hold the queue. It has the following constructor:

```
explicit stack(const Container &cnt = Container( ));
```

The **stack( )** constructor creates an empty stack. By default it uses a **deque** as a container, but a **stack** can only be accessed in a last-in, first-out manner. The container is held in a protected member called **c** of type **Container**.

The following comparison operators are defined for **stack**: ==, <, <=, !=, >, and >=.

14

stack contains the following member functions:

Member	**Description**
bool empty( ) const;	Returns true if the invoking stack is empty and false otherwise
void pop( );	Removes the top of the stack, which is technically the last element in the container
void push(const T &*val*);	Pushes an element onto the end of the stack. The last element in the container represents the top of the stack.
size_type size( ) const;	Returns the number of elements currently in the stack
value_type &top( ); const value_type &top( ) const;	Returns a reference to the top of the stack, which is the last element in the container. The element is not removed.

vector

The **vector** class supports a dynamic array. Its template specification is shown here:

template <class T, class Allocator = allocator<T>>
  class vector

Here, **T** is the type of data being stored, and **Allocator** specifies the allocator. It has the following constructors:

explicit vector(const Allocator &*a* = Allocator( ));

explicit vector(size_type *num*, const T &*val* = T ( ),
        const Allocator &*a* = Allocator( ));

vector(const vector<T, Allocator> &*ob*);

template <class InIter> vector(InIter *start*, InIter *end*,
        const Allocator &*a* = Allocator( ));

The first form constructs an empty vector. The second form constructs a vector that has *num* elements with the value *val*. The third form constructs a vector that contains the same elements as *ob*. The fourth form constructs a vector that contains the elements in the range specified by *start* and *end*.

The following comparison operators are defined for **vector**: ==, <, <=, !=, >, and >=.

vector contains the following member functions:

Member	Description
template <class InIter> void assign(InIter *start*, InIter *end*);	Assigns the vector the sequence defined by *start* and *end*
template <class Size, class T> void assign(Size *num*, const T &*val* = T( ));	Assigns the vector *num* elements of value *val*
reference at(size_type *i*); const_reference at(size_type *i*) const;	Returns a reference to an element specified by *i*
reference back( ); const_reference back( ) const;	Returns a reference to the last element in the vector
iterator begin( ); const_iterator begin( ) const;	Returns an iterator to the first element in the vector
size_type capacity( ) const;	Returns the current capacity of the vector. This is the number of elements it can hold before it will need to allocate more memory.
void clear( );	Removes all elements from the vector
bool empty( ) const;	Returns true if the invoking vector is empty and false otherwise
iterator end( ); const_iterator end( ) const;	Returns an iterator to the end of the vector
iterator erase(iterator *i*);	Removes the element pointed to by *i*; returns an iterator to the element after the one removed

Member	Description
iterator erase(iterator *start*, iterator *end*);	Removes the elements in the range *start* to *end*; returns an iterator to the element after the last element removed
reference front( ); const_reference front( ) const;	Returns a reference to the first element in the vector
allocator_type get_allocator( ) const;	Returns vector's allocator
iterator insert(iterator *i*, const T &*val* = T( ));	Inserts *val* immediately before the element specified by *i*. An iterator to the element is returned.
void insert(iterator *i*, size_type *num*, const T &*val*);	Inserts *num* copies of *val* immediately before the element specified by *i*
template <class InIter> void insert(iterator *i*, InIter *start*, InIter *end*);	Inserts the sequence defined by *start* and *end* immediately before the element specified by *i*
size_type max_size( ) const;	Returns the maximum number of elements that the vector can hold
reference operator[ ](size_type *i*) const; const_reference operator[ ](size_type *i*) const;	Returns a reference to the element specified by *i*
void pop_back( );	Removes the last element in the vector
void push_back(const T &*val*);	Adds an element with the value specified by *val* to the end of the vector
reverse_iterator rbegin( ); const_reverse_iterator rbegin( ) const;	Returns a reverse iterator to the end of the vector
reverse_iterator rend( ); const_reverse_iterator rend( ) const;	Returns a reverse iterator to the start of the vector
void reserve(size_type *num*);	Sets the capacity of the vector so that it is equal to at least *num*

Member	**Description**
void resize(size_type *num*, T *val* = T ( ));	Changes the size of the vector to that specified by *num*. If the vector must be lengthened, then elements with the value specified by *val* are added to the end.
size_type size( ) const;	Returns the number of elements current in the vector
void swap(vector<T, Allocator> &*ob*);	Exchanges the elements stored in the invoking vector with those in *ob*

The STL also contains a specialization of **vector** for Boolean values. It includes all of the functionality of **vector** and adds these two members:

void flip( );	Reverses all bits in the vector
static void swap(reference *i*, reference *j*);	Exchanges the bits specified by *i* and *j*

Algorithms

The standard algorithms are described here.

All of the algorithms are template functions. To simplify the descriptions, the template specification will not be shown. Instead, the descriptions will use the following generic type names, throughout:

Generic Name	**Represents**
BiIter	Bidirectional iterator
ForIter	Forward iterator
InIter	Input iterator
OutIter	Output iterator
RandIter	Random access iterator
T	Some type of data

Generic Name	Represents
Size	Some type of integer
Func	Some type of function
Generator	A function that generates objects
BinPred	Binary predicate
UnPred	Unary predicate
Comp	Comparison function that returns the result of arg1 < arg2

adjacent_find

```
ForIter adjacent_find(ForIter start, ForIter end);
ForIter adjacent_find(ForIter start, ForIter end,
                      BinPred pfn);
```

The **adjacent_find( )** algorithm searches for adjacent matching elements within a sequence specified by *start* and *end* and returns an iterator to the first element. If no adjacent pair is found, *end* is returned. The first version looks for equivalent elements. The second version lets you specify your own method for determining matching elements.

binary_search

```
bool binary_search(ForIter start, ForIter end,
                   const T &val);
bool binary_search(ForIter start, ForIter end,
                   const T &val, Comp cmpfn);
```

The **binary_search( )** algorithm performs a binary search on an ordered sequence beginning at *start* and ending with *end* for the value specified by *val*. It returns true if *val* is found and false otherwise. The first version compares the elements in the specified sequence for equality. The second version allows you to specify your own comparison function.

copy

```
OutIter copy(InIter start, InIter end, OutIter result);
```

The **copy( )** algorithm copies a sequence beginning at *start* and ending with *end*, putting the result into the sequence pointed to by *result*. It returns a pointer to the end of the resulting sequence. The range to be copied must not overlap with *result*.

copy_backward

```
BiIter2 copy_backward(BiIter1 start, BiIter1 end,
                      BiIter2 result);
```

The **copy_backward( )** algorithm is the same as **copy( )** except that it moves the elements from the end of the sequence first.

count

```
size_t count(InIter start, InIter end, const T &val);
```

The **count( )** algorithm returns the number of elements in the sequence beginning at *start* and ending at *end* that match *val*.

count_if

```
size_t count(InIter start, InIter end, UnPred pfn);
```

The **count_if( )** algorithm returns the number of elements in the sequence beginning at *start* and ending at *end* for which the unary predicate *pfn* returns true.

equal

```
bool equal(InIter1 start1, InIter1 end1, InIter2 start2);
```

The **equal( )** algorithm determines if two ranges are the same. The range determined by *start1* and *end1* is tested against the sequence pointed to by *start2*. If the ranges are the same, true is returned. Otherwise, false is returned.

equal_range

```
pair<ForIter, ForIter> equal_range(ForIter start,
                                    ForIter end,
                                    const T &val);
pair<ForIter, ForIter> equal_range(ForIter start,
                                    ForIter end,
                                    const T &val,
                                    Comp cmpfn);
```

The **equal_range( )** algorithm returns a range in which an element can be inserted into a sequence without disrupting the ordering of the sequence. The region in which to search for such a range is specified by *start* and *end*. The value is passed in *val*. To specify your own search criteria, specify the comparison function *cmpfn*.

The template class **pair** is a utility class that can hold a pair of objects in its **first** and **second** members.

fill and fill_n

```
void fill(ForIter start, ForIter end, const T &val);
void fill_n(ForIter start, Size num, const T &val);
```

The **fill( )** and **fill_n( )** algorithms fill a range with the value specified by *val*. For **fill( )** the range is specified by *start* and *end*. For **fill_n( )**, the range begins at *start* and runs for *num* elements.

find

```
InIter find(InIter start, InIter end, const T &val);
```

The **find( )** algorithm searches the range *start* to *end* for the value specified by *val*. It returns an iterator to the first occurrence of the element or to *end* if the value is not in the sequence.

find_end

```
FwdIter1 find_end(ForIter1 start1, ForIter1 end1,
                  ForIter2 start2, ForIter2 end2);
FwdIter1 find_end(ForIter1 start1, ForIter1 end1,
                  ForIter2 start2, ForIter2 end2,
                  BinPred pfn);
```

The **find_end( )** algorithm finds the last iterator of the subsequence defined by *start2* and *end2* within the range *start1* and *end1*. If the sequence is found, an iterator to the last element in the sequence is returned. Otherwise, the iterator *end1* is returned.

The second form allows you to specify a binary predicate that determines when elements match.

14

find_first_of

```
FwdIter1 find_first_of(ForIter1 start1, ForIter1 end1,
                       ForIter2 start2, ForIter2 end2);
FwdIter1 find_first_of(ForIter1 start1, ForIter1 end1,
                       ForIter2 start2, ForIter2 end2,
                       BinPred pfn);
```

The **find_first_of( )** algorithm finds the first element within the sequence defined by *start1* and *end1* that matches an element within the range *start2* and *end2*. If no matching element is found, the iterator *end1* is returned.

The second form allows you to specify a binary predicate that determines when elements match.

find_if

```
InIter find_if(InIter start, InIter end, UnPred pfn);
```

The **find( )** algorithm searches the range *start* to *end* for an element for which the unary predicate *pfn* returns true. It returns an iterator to the first occurrence of the element or to *end* if the value is not in the sequence.

for_each

```
Func for_each(InIter start, InIter end, Func fn);
```

The **for_each( )** algorithm applies the function *fn* to the range of elements specified by *start* and *end*. It returns *fn*.

generate and generate_n

```
void generate(ForIter start, ForIter end, Generator fngen);
void generate_n(OutIter start, Size num, Generator fngen);
```

The algorithms **generate( )** and **generate_n( )** assign elements in a range of values returned by a generator function. For **generate( )**, the range being assigned is specified by *start* and *end*. For **generate_n( )**, the range begins at *start* and runs for *num* elements. The generator function is passed in *fngen*. It has no parameters.

includes

```
bool includes(InIter1 start1, InIter1 end1, InIter2 start2,
              InIter2 end2);
bool includes(InIter1 start1, InIter1 end1, InIter2 start2,
              InIter2 end2, Comp cmpfn);
```

The **includes( )** algorithm determines if the sequence defined by *start1* and *end1* includes all of the elements in the sequence defined by *start2* and *end2*. It returns true if the elements are all found and false otherwise.

The second form allows you to specify a comparison function that determines when one element is less than another.

inplace_merge

```
void inplace_merge(BiIter start, BiIter mid, BiIter end);
void inplace_merge(BiIter start, BiIter mid, BiIter end,
                   Comp cmpfn);
```

Within a single sequence, the **inplace_merge( )** algorithm merges the range defined by *start* and *mid* with the range defined by *mid* and *end*. Both ranges must be sorted in increasing order. After executing, the resulting sequence is sorted in increasing order.

The second form allows you to specify a comparison function that determines when one element is less than another.

iter_swap

```
void iter_swap(ForIter1 i, ForIter2 j);
```

The **iter_swap( )** algorithm exchanges the values pointed to by its two iterator arguments.

lexicographical_compare

```
bool lexicographical_compare(InIter1 start1, InIter1 end1,
                             InIter2 start2, InIter2 end2);
bool lexicographical_compare(InIter1 start1, InIter1 end1,
                             InIter2 start2, InIter2 end2,
                             Comp cmpfn);
```

The **lexicographical_compare( )** algorithm alphabetically compares the sequence defined by *start1* and *end1* with the sequence defined by *start2* and *end2*. It returns true if the first sequence is lexicographically less than the second. (That is, if the first sequence would come before the second using dictionary order.)

The second form allows you to specify a comparison function that determines when one element is less than another.

lower_bound

```
ForIter lower_bound(ForIter start, ForIter end,
                    const T &val);
ForIter lower_bound(ForIter start, ForIter end,
                    const T &val, Comp cmpfn);
```

The **lower_bound( )** algorithm finds the first point in the sequence defined by *start* and *end* that is not less than *val*. It returns an iterator to this point.

The second form allows you to specify a comparison function that determines when one element is less than another.

make_heap

```
void make_heap(RandIter start, RandIter end);
void make_heap(RandIter start, RandIter end, Comp cmpfn);
```

The **make_heap( )** algorithm constructs a heap from the sequence defined by *start* and *end*.

The second form allows you to specify a comparison function that determines when one element is less than another.

max

```
const T &max(const T &i, const T &j);
const T &max(const T &i, const T &j, Comp cmpfn);
```

The **max( )** algorithm returns the maximum of two values.

The second form allows you to specify a comparison function that determines when one element is less than another.

max_element

```
ForIter max_element(ForIter start, ForIter last);
ForIter max_element(ForIter start, ForIter last,
                    Comp cmpfn);
```

The **max_element( )** algorithm returns an iterator to the maximum element within the range *start* and *last*.

The second form allows you to specify a comparison function that determines when one element is less than another.

merge

```
OutIter merge(InIter1 start1, InIter1 end1, InIter2 start2,
              InIter2 end2, OutIter result);
OutIter merge(InIter1 start1, InIter1 end1, InIter2 start2,
              InIter2 end2, OutIter result, Comp cmpfn);
```

14

The **merge( )** algorithm merges two ordered sequences, placing the result into a third sequence. The sequences to be merged are defined by *start1*, *end1* and *start2*, *end2*. The result is put into the sequence pointed to by *result*. An iterator to the end of the resulting sequence is returned.

The second form allows you to specify a comparison function that determines when one element is less than another.

min

```
const T &min(const T &i, const T &j);
const T &min(const T &i, const T &j, Comp cmpfn);
```

The **min( )** algorithm returns the minimum of two values.

The second form allows you to specify a comparison function that determines when one element is less than another.

min_element

```
ForIter min_element(ForIter start, ForIter last);
ForIter min_element(ForIter start, ForIter last,
                    Comp cmpfn);
```

The **min_element( )** algorithm returns an iterator to the minimum element within the range *start* and *last*.

The second form allows you to specify a comparison function that determines when one element is less than another.

mismatch

```
pair<InIter1, InIter2> mismatch(InIter1 start1,
                                InIter1 end1,
                                InIter2 start2);
pair<InIter1, InIter2> mismatch(InIter1 start1,
                                InIter1 end1,
                                InIter2 start2,
                                BinPred pfn);
```

The **mismatch( )** algorithm finds the first mismatch between the elements in two sequences. Iterators to the two elements are returned. If no mismatch is found, iterators to the last element in each sequence are returned.

The second form allows you to specify a binary predicate that determines when one element is equal to another.

The **pair** template class contains two data members called **first** and **second**, which hold the pair of values.

next_permutation

```
bool next_permutation(BiIter start, BiIter end);
bool next_permutation(BiIter start, BiIter end, Comp cmpfn);
```

The **next_permutation( )** algorithm constructs the next permutation of a sequence. The permutations are generated assuming a sorted sequence from low to high represents the first permutation. If the next permutation does not exist, **next_permutation( )** sorts the sequence as its first permutation and returns false. Otherwise, it returns true.

The second form allows you to specify a comparison function that determines when one element is less than another.

nth_element

```
void nth_element(RandIter start, RandIter element,
                 RandIter end);
void nth_element(RandIter start, RandIter element,
                 RandIter end, Comp cmpfn);
```

The **nth_element( )** algorithm arranges the sequence specified by *start* and *end* such that all elements less than *element* come before that element and all elements greater than *element* come after it.

The second form allows you to specify a comparison function that determines when one element is greater than another.

partial_sort

```
void partial_sort(RandIter start, RandIter mid,
                  RandIter end);
void partial_sort(RandIter start, RandIter mid,
                  RandIter end, Comp cmpfn);
```

The **partial_sort( )** algorithm sorts the range *start* to *end*. However, after execution, only elements in the range *start* to *mid* will be in sorted order.

The second form allows you to specify a comparison function that determines when one element is less than another.

partial_sort_copy

```
RandIter partial_sort_copy(InIter start, InIter end,
                           RandIter res_start,
                           RandIter res_end);
RandIter partial_sort_copy(InIter start, InIter end,
                           RandIter res_start,
                           RandIter res_end, Comp cmpfn);
```

The **partial_sort_copy( )** algorithm sorts the range *start* to *end* and then copies as many elements as will fit into the result sequence defined by *res_start* and *res_end*. It returns an iterator to the last element copied into the result sequence.

The second form allows you to specify a comparison function that determines when one element is less than another.

partition

```
BiIter partition(BiIter start, BiIter end, UnPred pfn);
```

The **partition( )** algorithm arranges the sequence defined by *start* and *end* such that all elements for which the predicate specified by *pfn* returns true come before those for which the predicate returns false. It returns an iterator to the beginning of the elements for which the predicate is false.

pop_heap

```
void pop_heap(RandIter start, RandIter end);
void pop_heap(RandIter start, RandIter end, Comp cmpfn);
```

The **pop_heap( )** algorithm exchanges the *first* and *last* −1 elements and then rebuilds the heap.

The second form allows you to specify a comparison function that determines when one element is less than another.

prev_permutation

```
bool prev_permutation(BiIter start, BiIter end);
bool prev_permutation(BiIter start, BiIter end,
                      Comp cmpfn);
```

The **prev_permutation( )** algorithm constructs previous permutations of a sequence. The permutations are generated assuming a sorted sequence from low to high represents the first permutation. If the previous permutation does not exist, **prev_permutation( )** sorts the sequence as its final permutation and returns false. Otherwise, it returns true.

The second form allows you to specify a comparison function that determines when one element is less than another.

push_heap

```
void push_heap(RandIter start, RandIter end);
void push_heap(RandIter start, RandIter end, Comp cmpfn);
```

The **push_heap( )** algorithm pushes an element onto the end of a heap. The range specified by *start* and *end* is assumed to represent a valid heap.

The second form allows you to specify a comparison function that determines when one element is less than another.

random_shuffle

```
void random_shuffle(RandIter start, RandIter end);
void random_shuffle(RandIter start, RandIter end,
                    Generator rand_gen);
```

The **random_shuffle( )** algorithm randomizes the sequence defined by *start* and *end*.

The second form specifies a custom random number generator. This function must have the following general form:

rand_gen(*num*);

It must return a random number between 0 and *num*.

remove, remove_if, remove_copy, and remove_copy_if

```
ForIter remove(ForIter start, ForIter end, const T &val);
ForIter remove_if(ForIter start, ForIter end, UnPred pfn);
OutIter remove_copy(InIter start, InIter end,
                    OutIter result, const T &val);
OutIter remove_copy_if(InIter start, InIter end,
                       OutIter result, UnPred pfn);
```

The **remove( )** algorithm removes elements from the specified range that are equal to *val*. It returns an iterator to the end of the remaining elements.

The **remove_if( )** algorithm removes elements from the specified range for which the predicate *pfn* is true. It returns an iterator to the end of the remaining elements.

The **remove_copy( )** algorithm copies elements from the specified range that are equal to *val* and puts the result into the sequence pointed to by *result*. It returns an iterator to the end of the result.

The **remove_copy_if( )** algorithm copies elements from the specified range for which the predicate *pfn* is true and puts the result into the sequence pointed to by *result*. It returns an iterator to the end of the result.

replace, replace_copy, replace_if, and replace_copy_if

```
void replace(ForIter start, ForIter end, const T &old,
          Const T &new);
void replace_if(ForIter start, ForIter end, UnPred pfn,
             Const T &new);
OutIter replace_copy(InIter start, InIter end,
                  OutIter result, const T &old,
                  Const T &new);
OutIter replace_copy_if(InIter start, InIter end,
                     OutIter result, UnPred pfn,
                     Const T &new);
```


Within the specified range, the **replace( )** algorithm replaces elements that have the value *old* with elements that have the value *new*.

Within the specified range, the **replace_if( )** algorithm replaces those elements for which the predicate *pfn* is true with elements that have the value *new*.

Within the specified range, the **replace_copy( )** algorithm copies elements to *result*. In the process it replaces elements that have the value *old* with elements that have the value *new*. The original range is unchanged. An iterator to the end of *result* is returned.

Within the specified range, the **replace_copy_if( )** algorithm copies elements to *result*. In the process it replaces elements for which the predicate *pfn* returns true with elements that have the value *new*. The original range is unchanged. An iterator to the end of *result* is returned.

reverse and reverse_copy

```
void reverse(BiIter start, BiIter end);
OutIter reverse_copy(BiIter first, BiIter last,
                     OutIter result);
```

The **reverse( )** algorithm reverses the order of the range specified by *start* and *end.*

The **reverse_copy( )** algorithm copies in reverse order the range specified by *start* and *end* and stores the result in *result.* It returns an iterator to the end of *result.*

rotate and rotate_copy

```
void rotate(ForIter start, ForIter mid, ForIter end);
OutIter rotate_copy(ForIter start, ForIter mid, ForIter end
                   OutIter result);
```

The **rotate( )** algorithm left rotates the elements in the range specified by *start* and *end* so that the element specified by *mid* becomes the new first element.

The **rotate_copy( )** algorithm copies the range specified by *start* and *end,* storing the result in *result.* In the process it left rotates the elements so that the element specified by *mid* becomes the new first element. It returns an iterator to the end of *result.*

search

```
ForIter1 search(ForIter1 start1, ForIter1 end1,
                ForIter2 start2, ForIter2 end2);
ForIter1 search(ForIter1 start1, ForIter1 end1,
                ForIter2 start2, ForIter2 end2,
                BinPred pfn);
```

The **search( )** algorithm searches for a subsequence within a sequence. The sequence being searched is defined by *start1* and *end1.* The subsequence being sought is specified by *start2* and *end2.* If the subsequence is found, an iterator to its beginning is returned. Otherwise, *end1* is returned.

The second form allows you to specify a binary predicate that determines when one element is equal to another.

search_n

```
ForIter search_n(ForIter start, ForIter end, Size num,
                 Const T &val);
ForIter search_n(ForIter start, ForIter end, Size num,
                 Const T &val, BinPred pfn);
```


The **search_n( )** algorithm searches for a sequence of *num* similar elements within a sequence. The sequence being searched is defined by *start1* and *end1*. If the subsequence is found, an iterator to its beginning is returned. Otherwise, *end* is returned.

The second form allows you to specify a binary predicate that determines when one element is equal to another.

set_difference

```
OutIter set_difference(InIter1 start1, InIter1 end1,
                       InIter2 start2, InIter2 end2,
                       OutIter result);
OutIter set_difference(InIter1 start1, InIter1 end1,
                       InIter2 start2, InIter2 end2,
                       OutIter result, Comp cmpfn);
```

The **set_difference( )** algorithm produces a sequence that contains the difference between the two ordered sets defined by *start1*, *end1* and *start2*, *end2*. That is, the set defined by *start2*, *end2* is subtracted from the set defined by *start1*, *end1*. The result is ordered and put into *result*. It returns an iterator to the end of the result.

The second form allows you to specify a comparison function that determines when one element is less than another.

set_intersection

```
OutIter set_intersection(InIter1 start1, InIter1 end1,
                         InIter2 start2, InIter2 end2,
                         OutIter result);
OutIter set_intersection(InIter1 start1, InIter1 end1,
                         InIter2 start2, InIter2 end2,
                         OutIter result, Comp cmpfn);
```

The **set_intersection( )** algorithm produces a sequence that contains the intersection of the two ordered sets defined by *start1*, *end1* and *start2*, *end2*. These are the elements found in both the sets. The result is ordered and put into *result*. It returns an iterator to the end of the result.

The second form allows you to specify a comparison function that determines when one element is less than another.

set_symmetric_difference

```
OutIter set_symmetric_difference(InIter1 start1,
                                 InIter1 end1,
                                 InIter2 start2,
                                 InIter2 end2,
                                 OutIter result);
OutIter set_symmetric_difference(InIter1 start1,
                                 InIter1 end1,
                                 InIter2 start2,
                                 InIter2 end2,
                                 OutIter result,
                                 Comp cmpfn);
```

The **set_symmetric_difference( )** algorithm produces a sequence that contains the symmetric difference between the two ordered sets defined by *start1*, *end1* and *start2*, *end2*. That is, the resultant set contains only those elements that are not common to both sets. The result is ordered and put into *result.* It returns an iterator to the end of the result.

The second form allows you to specify a comparison function that determines when one element is less than another.

set_union

```
OutIter set_union(InIter1 start1, InIter1 end1,
                  InIter2 start2, InIter2 end2,
                  OutIter result);
OutIter set_union(InIter1 start1, InIter1 end1,
                  InIter2 start2, InIter2 end2,
                  OutIter result, Comp cmpfn);
```

14

The **set_union( )** algorithm produces a sequence that contains the union of the two ordered sets defined by *start1*, *end1* and *start2*, *end2*. Thus, the resultant set contains those elements that are in both sets. The result is ordered and put into *result.* It returns an iterator to the end of the result.

The second form allows you to specify a comparison function that determines when one element is less than another.

sort

```
void sort(RandIter start, RandIter end);
void sort(RandIter start, RandIter end, Comp cmpfn);
```

The **sort( )** algorithm sorts the range specified by *start* and *end.*

The second form allows you to specify a comparison function that determines when one element is less than another.

sort_heap

```
void sort_heap(RandIter start, RandIter end);
void sort_heap(RandIter start, RandIter end, Comp cmpfn);
```

The **sort_heap( )** algorithm sorts a heap within the range specified by *start* and *end.*

The second form allows you to specify a comparison function that determines when one element is less than another.

stable_partition

```
BiIter stable_partition(BiIter start, BiIter end,
                        BinPred pfn);
```

The **stable_partition( )** algorithm arranges the sequence defined by *start* and *end* such that all elements for which the predicate specified by *pfn* returns true come before those for which the predicate returns false. The partitioning is stable. This means that the relative ordering of the sequence is preserved. It returns an iterator to the beginning of the elements for which the predicate is false.

stable_sort

```
void stable_sort(RandIter start, RandIter end);
void stable_sort(RandIter start, RandIter end,
                 Comp cmpfn);
```

The **sort( )** algorithm sorts the range specified by *start* and *end*. The sort is stable. This means that equal elements are not rearranged.

The second form allows you to specify a comparison function that determines when one element is less than another.

swap

```
void swap(T &i, T &j);
```

The **swap( )** algorithm exchanges the values referred to by *i* and *j*.

swap_ranges

```
ForIter2 swap_ranges(ForIter1 start1, ForIter1 end1,
                     ForIter2 start2);
```

The **swap_ranges( )** algorithm exchanges elements in the range specified by *start1* and *end1* with elements in the sequence beginning at *start2*. It returns a pointer to the end of the sequence specified by *start2*.

transform

```
OutIter transform(InIter start, InIter end,
                  OutIter result, Func unaryfunc);
OutIter transform(InIter1 start1, InIter1 end1,
                  InIter2 start2, OutIter result,
                  Func binaryfunc);
```

The **transform( )** algorithm applies a function to a range of elements and stores the outcome in *result.* In the first form, the range is specified by *start* and *end.* The function to be applied is specified by *unaryfunc.* This function receives the value of an element in its parameter and it must return its transformation.

In the second form, the transformation is applied using a binary operator function that receives the value of an element from the sequence to be transformed in its first parameter and an element from the second sequence as its second parameter.

Both versions return an iterator to the end of the resulting sequence.

Programming Tip

One of the more interesting algorithms is **transform( )**, because it modifies each element in a range according to a function that you provide. For example, the following program uses a simple transformation function called **xform( )** to square the contents of a list. Notice that the resulting sequence is stored in the same list that provided the original sequence.

```
// An example of the transform algorithm.
#include <iostream>
#include <list>
#include <algorithm>
using namespace std;

// A simple transformation function.
int xform(int i) {
  return i * i; // square original value
}
```

```
int main()
{
  list<int> xl;
  int i;

  // put values into list
  for(i=0; i<10; i++) xl.push_back(i);

  cout << "Original contents of xl: ";
  list<int>::iterator p = xl.begin();
  while(p != xl.end()) {
    cout << *p << " ";
    p++;
  }

  cout << endl;

  // transform xl
  p = transform(xl.begin(), xl.end(), xl.begin(),
                xform);

  cout << "Transformed contents of xl: ";
  p = xl.begin();
  while(p != xl.end()) {
    cout << *p << " ";
    p++;
  }

  return 0;
}
```

The output produced by the program is shown here:

```
Original contents of xl: 0 1 2 3 4 5 6 7 8 9
Transformed contents of xl: 0 1 4 9 16 25 36 49 64 81
```

As you can see, each element in the **xl** has been squared.

unique and unique_copy

```
ForIter unique(ForIter start, ForIter end);
ForIter unique(ForIter start, ForIter end, BinPred pfn);
OutIter unique_copy(ForIter start, ForIter end,
                    OutIter result);
OutIter unique_copy(ForIter start, ForIter end,
                    OutIter result, BinPred pfn);
```

The **unique( )** algorithm eliminates duplicate elements from the specified range. The second form allows you to specify a binary predicate that determines when one element is equal to another. **unique( )** returns an iterator to the end of the range.

The **unique_copy( )** algorithm copies the range specified by *start1* and *end1*, eliminating duplicate elements in the process. The outcome is put into *result.* The second form allows you to specify a binary predicate that determines when one element is equal to another. **unique_copy( )** returns an iterator to the end of the range.

upper_bound

```
ForIter upper_bound(ForIter start, ForIter end,
                    const T &val);
ForIter upper_bound(ForIter start, ForIter end,
                    const T &val, Comp cmpfn);
```

The **upper_bound( )** algorithm finds the last point in the sequence defined by *start* and *end* that is not greater than *val.* It returns an iterator to this point.

The second form allows you to specify a comparison function that determines when one element is less than another.

Chapter 15—C++ Strings and Exceptions

In addition to the iostream library and the STL, the C++ standard library defines several other classes that handle a variety of situations. For example, there are classes that support numeric operations, complex arithmetic, and localization. While many of these classes are not typically used in day-to-day programming, two are: strings and exceptions. They are described here.

STRINGS

C++ supports character strings two ways. The first is as a null-terminated character array. This is sometimes referred to as a C-string. The second way is as a class object of type **basic_string**. There are two specializations of **basic_string**: **string**, which supports character strings, and **wstring**, which supports wide-character strings. Most often, you will use string objects of type **string** and they are examined, here.

A class used by **basic_string** is **char_traits**, which defines several attributes of the characters that comprise a string. It is important to understand that while the most common strings are made up of either **char** or **wchar_t** characters, **basic_string** can operate on any object that can be used to represent a text character.

The **basic_string** class is essentially a container. This means that it supports the algorithms described in the STL section. However, strings have additional capabilities. To use **string** objects you must include **<string>**.

The template specification for **basic_string** is

```
template <class charT, class Traits = char_traits<charT>,
          class Allocator = allocator<T>> class basic_string
```

Here, **charT** is the type of character being used, **Traits** is the class that describes the characters, and **Allocator** specifies the allocator. It has the following constructors:

```
explicit basic_string(const Allocator &a = Allocator( ));

basic_string(size_type len, charT ch,
             const Allocator &a = Allocator( ));

basic_string(const charT *str; const Allocator &a =
             Allocator( ));

basic_string(const charT *str; size_type len,
             const Allocator &a = Allocator( ));

basic_string(const basic_string &str, size_type indx = 0,
             size_type len, const Allocator &a =
             Allocator( ));

template <class InIter> basic_string(InIter start,
           InIter end, const Allocator &a = Allocator( ));
```

The first form constructs an empty string. The second form constructs a string that has *len* characters of value *ch*. The third form constructs a string that contains the same elements as *str*. The fourth form constructs a string that contains a substring of *str* that begins at 0 and is *len* characters long. The fifth form constructs a string from another **basic_string** using the substring that begins at *indx* that is *len* characters long. The sixth form constructs a string that contains the elements in the range specified by *start* and *end*.

The following comparison operators are defined for **basic_string**: ==, <, <=, !=, >, and >=.

Also defined is the + operator, which yields the result of concatenating one string with another, and the I/O operators << and >>, which can be used to input and output strings.

The + operator can be used to concatenate a string object with another string object or a string object with a C-style string. That is, the following variations are supported:

string + string

string + C-string

C-string + string

The + operator can also be used to concatenate a character onto the end of a string.

The **basic_string** class defines the constant **npos**, which is usually −1. This constant represents the length of the longest possible string.

In the descriptions, the generic type **charT** represents the type of character stored by a string. Since the names of the placeholder types in a template class are arbitrary, the container classes declare **typedef**ed versions of these types. This makes the type names concrete. The commonly used types defined by **basic_string** are listed here:

size_type	Some integral type equivalent to **size_t**
reference	A reference to a character
const_reference	A **const** reference to a character
iterator	An iterator
const_iterator	A **const** iterator
reverse_iterator	A reverse iterator
const_reverse_iterator	A **const** reverse iterator
value_type	The type of character stored in a string

allocator_type	The type of the allocator
pointer	A pointer to a character within a string
const_pointer	A **const** pointer to a character within a string

basic_string contains the following member functions:

Member	**Description**
basic_string &append(const basic_string &*str*);	Appends *str* onto the end of the invoking string; returns ***this**
basic_string &append(const basic_string &*str*, size_type *indx*, size_type *len*);	Appends a substring of *str* onto the end of the invoking string. The substring being appended begins at *indx* and runs for *len* characters; returns ***this**
basic_string &append(const charT **str*);	Appends *str* onto the end of the invoking string; returns * **this**.
basic_string &append(const charT **str*, size_type *num*);	Appends the first *num* characters from *str* onto the end of the invoking string; returns ***this**
basic_string &append(size_type *len*, char T *ch*);	Appends *len* characters specified by *ch* onto the end of the invoking string; returns ***this**
template<class InIter> basic_string &append(InIter *start*, InIter *end*);	Appends the sequence specified by *start* and *end* onto the end of the invoking string; returns ***this**
basic_string &assign(const basic_string &*str*);	Assigns *str* to the invoking string; returns ***this**
basic_string &assign(const basic_string &str, size_type *indx*, size_type *len*);	Assigns a substring of *str* to the invoking string. The substring being assigned begins at *indx* and runs for *len* characters. Returns ***this**.
basic_string &assign(const charT **str*);	Assigns *str* to the invoking string; returns ***this**
basic_string &assign(const charT **str*, size_type *len*);	Assigns the first *len* character from *str* to the invoking string; returns ***this**

Member	**Description**
basic_string &assign(size_type *len*, char T *ch*);	Assigns *len* characters specified by *ch* to the end of the invoking string; returns ***this**
template<class InIter> basic_string &append(InIter *start*, InIter *end*);	Assigns the sequence specified by *start* and *end* to the invoking string; returns ***this**
reference at(size_type *indx*); const_reference at(size_type *indx*) const;	Returns a reference to the character specified by *indx*
iterator begin( ); const_iterator begin( ) const;	Returns an iterator to the first element in the string
const charT *c_str( ) const;	Returns a pointer to a C-style (i.e., null-terminated) version of the invoking string
size_type capacity( ) const;	Returns the current capacity of the string. This is the number of characters it can hold before it will need to allocate more memory.
int compare (const basic_string &*str*) const;	Compares *str* to the invoking string. It returns one of the following: Less than 0 if ***this** < *str* 0 if ***this** == *str* Greater than 0 if ***this** > *str*
int compare(size_type *indx*, size_type *len*, const basic_string &*str*) const;	Compares *str* to a substring within the invoking string. The substring begins a *indx* and is *len* characters long. It returns one of the following: Less than 0 if ***this** < *str* 0 if ***this** == *str* Greater than 0 if ***this** > *str*

Member	Description
int compare(size_type indx, size_type len, const basic_string &str, size_type indx2, size_type len2) const;	Compares a substring of str to a substring within the invoking string. The substring in the invoking string begins at indx and is len characters long. The substring in str begins at indx2 and is len2 characters long. It returns one of the following: Less than 0 if *this < str 0 if *this == str Greater than 0 if *this > str
int compare(const char T *str) const;	Compares str to the invoking string. It returns one of the following: Less than 0 if *this < str 0 if *this == str Greater than 0 if *this > str
int compare(size_type indx, size_type len, const char T *str, size_type len2 = npos) const;	Compares a substring of str to a substring within the invoking string. The substring in the invoking string begins at indx and is len characters long. The substring in str begins at 0 and is len2 characters long. It returns one of the following: Less than 0 if *this < str 0 if *this == str Greater than 0 if *this > str
size_type copy(charT *str, size_type len, size_type indx = 0) const;	Beginning at indx, copies len characters from the invoking string into the character array pointed to by str; returns the number of characters copied
const charT *data( ) const;	Returns a pointer to the first character in the invoking string
bool empty( ) const;	Returns true if the invoking string is empty and false otherwise
iterator end( ); const_iterator end( ) const;	Returns an iterator to the end of the string
iterator erase(iterator i);	Removes character pointed to by i; returns an iterator to the character after the one removed

Member	Description
iterator erase(iterator *start*, iterator *end*);	Removes characters in the range *start* to *end*; returns an iterator to the character after the last character removed
basic_string & erase(size_type *indx* = 0, size_type *len* = npos);	Beginning at *indx*, removes *len* characters from the invoking string; returns ***this**
size_type find(const basic_string &*str*, size_type *indx* = 0) const;	Returns the index of the first occurrence of *str* within the invoking string. The search begins at index *indx*. **npos** is returned if no match is found.
size_type find(const charT **str*, size_type *indx* = 0) const;	Returns the index of the first occurrence of *str* within the invoking string. The search begins at index *indx*. **npos** is returned if no match is found.
size_type find(const charT **str*, size_type *indx*, size_type *len*) const;	Returns the index of the first occurrence of the first *len* characters of *str* within the invoking string. The search begins at index *indx*. **npos** is returned if no match is found.
size_type find(charT *ch*, size_type *indx* = 0) const;	Returns the index of the first occurrence of *ch* within the invoking string. The search begins at index *indx*. **npos** is returned if no match is found.
size_type find_first_of(const basic_string &*str*, size_type *indx* = 0) const;	Returns the index of the first character within the invoking string that matches any character in *str*. The search begins at index *indx*. **npos** is returned if no match is found.
size_type find_first_of(const charT **str*, size_type *indx* = 0) const;	Returns the index of the first character within the invoking string that matches any character in *str*. The search begins at index *indx*. **npos** is returned if no match is found.

Member	Description
size_type find_first_of(const charT **str*, size_type *indx*, size_type *len*) const;	Returns the index of the first character within the invoking string that matches any character in the first *len* characters of *str*. The search begins at index *indx*. **npos** is returned if no match is found.
size_type find_first_of(charT *ch*, size_type *indx* = 0) const;	Returns the index of the first occurrence of *ch* within the invoking string. The search begins at index *indx*. **npos** is returned if no match is found.
size_type find_first_not_of(const basic_string &*str*, size_type *indx* = 0) const;	Returns the index of the first character within the invoking string that does not match any character in *str*. The search begins at index *indx*. **npos** is returned if no mismatch is found.
size_type find_first_not_of(const charT **str*, size_type *indx* = 0) const;	Returns the index of the first character within the invoking string that does not match any character in *str*. The search begins at index *indx*. **npos** is returned if no mismatch is found.
size_type find_first_not_of(const charT **str*, size_type *indx*, size_type *len*) const;	Returns the index of the first character within the invoking string that does not match any character in the first *len* characters of *str*. The search begins at index *indx*. **npos** is returned if no mismatch is found.
size_type find_first_not_of(charT *ch*, size_type *indx* = 0) const;	Returns the index of the first character within the invoking string that does not match *ch*. The search begins at index *indx*. **npos** is returned if no mismatch is found.
size_type find_last_of(const basic_string &*str*, size_type *indx* = npos) const;	Returns the index of the last character within the invoking string that matches any character in *str*. The search begins at index *indx*. **npos** is returned if no match is found.

Member	Description
size_type find_last_of(const charT **str*, size_type *indx* = npos) const;	Returns the index of the last character within the invoking string that matches any character in *str.* The search begins at index *indx.* **npos** is returned if no match is found.
size_type find_last_of(const charT **str*, size_type *indx,* size_type *len*) const;	Returns the index of the last character within the invoking string that matches any character in the first *len* characters of *str.* The search begins at index *indx.* **npos** is returned if no match is found.
size_type find_last_of(charT *ch,* size_type *indx* = npos) const;	Returns the index of the last occurrence of *ch* within the invoking string. The search begins at index *indx.* **npos** is returned if no match is found.
size_type find_last_not_of(const basic_string &*str,* size_type *indx* = npos) const;	Returns the index of the last character within the invoking string that does not match any character in *str.* The search begins at index *indx.* **npos** is returned if no mismatch is found.
size_type find_last_not_of (const charT **str,* size_type *indx* = npos) const;	Returns the index of the last character within the invoking string that does not match any character in *str.* The search begins at index *indx.* **npos** is returned if no mismatch is found.
size_type find_last_not_of(const charT **str,* size_type *indx,* size_type *len*) const;	Returns the index of the last character within the invoking string that does not match any character in the first *len* characters of *str.* The search begins at index *indx.* **npos** is returned if no mismatch is found.
size_type find_last_not_of(charT *ch,* size_type *indx* = npos) const;	Returns the index of the last character within the invoking string that does not match *ch.* The search begins at index *indx.* **npos** is returned if no mismatch is found.

Member	Description
allocator_type get_allocator( ) const;	Returns the string's allocator
iterator insert(iterator *i*, const charT &*ch* = charT( ));	Inserts *ch* immediately before the character specified by *i*. An iterator to the character is returned.
basic_string &insert(size_type *indx*, const basic_string &*str*);	Inserts *str* into the invoking string at the index specified by *indx*; returns ***this**
basic_string &insert(size_type *indx1*, const basic_string &*str*, size_type *indx2*, size_type *len*);	Inserts a substring of *str* into the invoking string at the index specified by *indx1*. The substring begins at *indx2* and is *len* characters long. Returns ***this**.
basic_string &insert(size_type *indx*, const charT **str*);	Inserts *str* into the invoking string at the index specified by *indx*; returns ***this**
basic_string &insert(size_type *indx*, const charT **str*, size_type *len*);	Inserts the first *len* characters of *str* into the invoking string at the index specified by *indx*; returns ***this**
basic_string &insert(size_type *indx*, size_type *len*, charT *ch*);	Inserts *len* characters of value *ch* into the invoking string at the index specified by *indx*; returns ***this**
void insert(iterator *i*, size_type *len*, const charT &*ch*);	Inserts *len* copies of *ch* immediately before the element specified by *i*
template <class InIter> void insert(iterator *i*, InIter *start*, InIter *end*);	Inserts the sequence defined by *start* and *end* immediately before the element specified by *i*
size_type length( ) const;	Returns the number of characters in the string
size_type max_size( ) const;	Returns the maximum number of characters that the string can hold
reference operator [ ](size_type *indx*) const; const_reference operator[ ] (size_type *indx*) const;	Returns a reference to the character specified by *indx*

Member	Description

basic_string &operator=(const basic_string &*str*);
basic_string &operator=(const charT **str*);
basic_string &operator=(charT *ch*);
	Assigns the specified string or character to the invoking string; returns ***this**

basic_string &operator+=(const basic_string &*str*);
basic_string &operator+=(const charT **str*);
basic_string &operator+=(charT *ch*);
	Appends the specified string or character onto the end of the invoking string; returns ***this**

reverse_iterator rbegin( ); const_reverse_iterator rbegin( ) const;	Returns a reverse iterator to the end of the string
reverse_iterator rend( ); const_reverse_iterator rend( ) const;	Returns a reverse iterator to the start of the string.
basic_string &replace(size_type *indx*, size_type *len*, const basic_string &*str*);	Replaces up to *len* characters in the invoking string, beginning at *indx* with the string in *str*; returns ***this**
basic_string &replace(size_type *indx1*, size_type *len1*, const basic_string &*str*, size_type *indx2*, size_type *len2*);	Replaces up to *len1* characters in the invoking string beginning at *indx1* with the *len2* characters from the string in *str* that begin at *indx2*; returns ***this**
basic_string &replace(size_type *indx*, size_type *len*, const charT **str*);	Replaces up to *len* characters in the invoking string, beginning at *indx* with the string in *str*; returns ***this**
basic_string &replace(size_type *indx1*, size_type *len1*, const charT **str*, size_type *len2*);	Replaces up to *len1* characters in the invoking string beginning at *indx1* with the *len2* characters from the string in *str* that begins at *indx2*; returns ***this**

Member	Description
basic_string &replace(size_type *indx*, size_type *len1*, size_type *len2*, charT *ch*);	Replaces up to *len1* characters in the invoking string beginning at *indx* with *len2* characters specified by *ch*; returns ***this**
basic_string &replace(iterator *start*, iterator *end*, const basic_string &*str*);	Replaces the range specified by *start* and *end* with *str*; returns ***this**
basic_string &replace(iterator *start*, iterator *end*, const charT **str*);	Replaces the range specified by *start* and *end* with *str*; returns ***this**
basic_string &replace(iterator *start*, iterator *end*, const charT **str*, size_type *len*);	Replaces the range specified by *start* and *end* with the first *len* characters from *str*; returns ***this**
basic_string &replace(iterator *start*, iterator *end*, size_type *len*, charT *ch*);	Replaces the range specified by *start* and *end* with the *len* characters specified by *ch*; returns ***this**
template <class InIter> basic_string &replace(iterator *start1*, iterator *end1*, InIter *start2*, InIter *end2*);	Replaces the range specified by *start1* and *end1* with the characters specified by *start2* and *end2*; returns ***this**
void reserve(size_type *num* = 0);	Sets the capacity of the string so that it is equal to at least *num*
void resize(size_type *num*); void resize(size_type *num*, charT *ch*);	Changes the size of the string to that specified by *num*. If the string must be lengthened, then elements with the value specified by *ch* are added to the end.
size_type rfind(const basic_string &str, size_type *indx* = npos) const;	Returns the index of the last occurrence of *str* within the invoking string. The search begins at index *indx*. **npos** is returned if no match is found.

Member	Description
size_type rfind(const charT **str*, size_type *indx* = npos) const;	Returns the index of the last occurrence of *str* within the invoking string. The search begins at index *indx*. **npos** is returned if no match is found.
size_type rfind(const charT **str*, size_type *indx*, size_type *len*) const;	Returns the index of the last occurrence of the first *len* characters of *str* within the invoking string. The search begins at index *indx*. **npos** is returned if no match is found.
size_type rfind(charT *ch*, size_type *indx* = npos) const;	Returns the index of the last occurrence of *ch* within the invoking string. The search begins at index *indx*. **npos** is returned if no match is found.
size_type size( ) const;	Returns the number of characters currently in the string
basic_string substr(size_type *indx* = 0, size_type *len* = npos) const;	Returns a substring of *len* characters beginning at *indx* within the invoking string
void swap(basic_string &*str*);	Exchanges the characters stored in the invoking string with those in *ob*

Programming Tip

While the traditional, C-style strings have always been simple to use, the C++ string classes make string handling extraordinarily easy. For example, using **string** objects you can use the assignment operator to assign a quoted string to a **string**, the relational operators to compare strings, and a wide variety of string manipulation functions that make substring operations convenient. For example, consider the following program:

15

```
// Demonstrate strings.
#include <iostream>
#include <string>
using namespace std;

int main()
{
  string str1 = "abcdefghijklmnopqrstuvwxyz";
  string str2;
  string str3(str1);

  str2 = str1.substr(10, 5);

  cout << "str1: " << str1 << endl;
  cout << "str2: " << str2 << endl;
  cout << "str3: " << str3 << endl;

  str1.replace(5, 10, "");
  cout << "str1.replace(5, 10, \"\"): "
       << str1 << endl;

  str1 = "one";
  str2 = "two";
  str3 = "three";

  cout << "str1.compare(str2): ";
  cout << str1.compare(str2) << endl;

  if(str1<str2) cout << "str1 is less than str2\n";

  string str4 = str1 + " " + str2 + " " + str3;
  cout << "str4: " << str4 << endl;

  int i = str4.find("wo");
  cout << "str4.substr(i): " << str4.substr(i);

  return 0;
}
```

The output from the program is shown here:

```
str1: abcdefghijklmnopqrstuvwxyz
str2: klmno
str3: abcdefghijklmnopqrstuvwxyz
str1.replace(5, 10, ""): abcdepqrstuvwxyz
str1.compare(str2): -1
str1 is less than str2
str4: one two three
str4.substr(i): wo three
```

Notice the ease with which the string handling is accomplished. For example, the + is used to concatenate strings and the < is used to compare two strings. To accomplish these operations using C-style, null-terminated strings, less convenient calls to the **strcat( )** and **strcmp( )** functions would have been required. Because C++ **string** objects can be freely mixed with C-style null-terminated strings, there is no disadvantage to using them in your program—and there are considerable benefits to be gained.

EXCEPTIONS

The standard C++ library defines two headers that relate to exceptions: <**exception**> and <**stdexcept**>. Exceptions are used to report error conditions. Each header is examined here.

<exception>

15

The <**exception**> header defines classes, types, and functions that relate to exception handling. The classes defined by

<**exception**> are shown here:

Class	**Purpose**
exception	A base class for all exceptions defined by the C++ standard library
bad_exception	The type of exception thrown by the **unexpected**( ) function

The types defined by <**exception**> are

Type	**Meaning**
terminate_handler	typedef void (*terminate_handler) ( );
unexpected_handler	typedef void (*unexpected_handler) ( );

The functions are shown here:

Function	**Description**
terminate_handler set_terminate (terminate_handler *fn*) throw( );	Sets the function specified by *fn* as the terminate handler. A pointer to the old terminate handler is returned.
unexpected_handler set_unexpected (unexpected_handler *fn*) throw( );	Sets the function specified by *fn* as the unexpected handler. A pointer to the old unexpected handler is returned.
void terminate( );	Calls the terminate handler when a fatal exception is unhandled; calls **abort**( ) by default
bool uncaught_exception( );	Returns true if an exception is uncaught
void unexpected( );	Calls the unexpected exception handler when a function throws a disallowed exception. By default, **terminate**( ) is called.

<stdexcept>

The header **<stdexcept>** defines several standard exceptions which may be thrown by C++ library functions and/or the run-time system. There are two general types of exceptions defined by **<stdexcept>**: logic errors and runtime errors. Logic errors occur because of mistakes made by the programmer. Runtime errors occur because of mistakes in library functions or the runtime system and are beyond programmer control.

The standard exceptions defined by C++ caused by logic errors are derived from the base class **logic_error**. These exceptions are shown here:

Exception	**Meaning**
domain_error	Domain error occurred
invalid_argument	Invalid argument used in function call
length_error	An attempt was made to create an object that was too large.
out_of_range	An argument to a function was not in the required range.

The following runtime exceptions are derived from the base class **runtime_error**:

Exception	**Meaning**
overflow_error	Arithmetic overflow occurred
range_error	An internal range error occurred
underflow_error	An underflow occurred

INDEX

O

P